D1525115

OAK ISLAND
Curses, Codes & Secret Societies

OAK ISLAND
Curses, Codes &
Secret Societies

Written and published by
James A. McQuiston, FSA Scot
jamesamcquiston@gmail.com

Printed in the USA
All Rights Reserved
©2022

Recorded history is chaotic at best, much like viewing a tapestry from the back side.

Some say it's written by the winners. Others blame selective recall or hidden information – even a bias toward evidence that supports a predetermined answer.

All the sincere historian can do is gather the seemingly endless threads, align them to documented time lines, tint them with possible motives, verify them with whatever science is available, and then spin them into an honest, logical yarn.

In the legal world this is called "Relative Plausibility." I call it my best attempt to bring at least some order to the chaos that is often found in the course of Oak Island research.

–James A. McQuiston, FSA Scot

This publication is designed to provide accurate information and credible theories concerning the history of Oak Island, Nova Scotia, and represents the culmination of years of research, interviews, presentations and visits to Oak Island. Every attempt has been made to verify information contained herein. However, the author and publisher makes no representation in regard to the completeness or accuracy of the information and accepts no liability of any kind alleged to be caused, directly or indirectly, from this book.

The author may be contacted at jamesamcquiston@gmail.com

TABLE OF CONTENTS

PREFACE

For the last seven years I've worked closely with a team of treasure hunters on a small island just off the coast of Nova Scotia known as Oak Island. I've appeared on the History Channel's popular cable TV shows *The Curse of Oak Island* and *The Curse of Oak Island: Drilling Down* about a dozen times. In addition, I have deeply studied several of the theories and the extraordinary circumstances that have surrounded this search for treasure that has taken place for over two centuries on an otherwise ordinary yet beautiful piece of ground.

As I carried out my Oak Island research I came upon my own theory for the source of the treasure that seems to be gaining traction. In fact, Rick Lagina, one of the lead searchers, made the statement on air during the 2020-21 season: "When you ask the who, what, when, where, why and how, I think James, above all the others, really deals with that... I can tell you what, James is not giving up." I guess this book is proof of that.

During the 2021 dig season I appeared for a sixth time in the Oak Island War Room presenting a new and unique theory concerning the so-called "90′ Stone." This meeting took place in the midst of the Covid crisis, which presented its own set of challenges.

I also had a long, private visit with Rick Lagina at his nearby home, learning many interesting things about his life and about the true state of affairs on Oak Island.

My overall theory revolves around a personal treasure that was stolen in October of 1622. It seems the theft of this treasure may have actually been the fulfillment of a different historic curse and this got me thinking about curses that appear to have come true over the years.

I've added to this tale some new information about specific secret societies that are rumored to have been involved in the burying of a treasure on Oak Island, plus my own unique take on the translation and purpose of the 90′ Stone found on Oak Island. This book presents information that I shared with the Oak Island team during the 2021 dig season and much more.

I have been aided in my research greatly because of a fellowship I enjoy with the Society of Antiquaries of Scotland, based in Edinburgh, Scotland. This small, elite organization of historians has been around since 1780.

My fellowship has given me valuable access to the National Museum of Scotland and the National Records of Scotland, and has made my introduction to other historical institutions like the British Museum and the National Archives of the UK much easier. I am also a member of the Royal Nova Scotia Historical Society.

In addition to this wonderful experience of exploring Scottish history and the Oak Island story, in my earlier years I also attended formal classes over a four year period, plus yearly refreshers for the next eight years, in subjects some folks might call alternative.

These classes focused on intuition and meditation. While I could write an entire book just on these subjects, suffice it to say that I have had my eyes opened considerably to the power of intention and the good it can reap or the havoc it can sow in a world where the true reason behind events is so often hidden.

Having traveled this path helped me to understand why I seem to continually receive the assistance I need, usually at just the right time, while writing my books.

We are often told to "pay attention" (which is very important) but it's seldom ever mentioned that we need to apply "intention" to our tasks in order to reap amazing and sometimes unexpected results.

One of the best anecdotes that explains what I am speaking of concerns an episode that happened on one of my many trips to Oak Island.

During a break in the action on the island I stopped into a used book store in Lunenburg, a town not far from Oak Island. One thing that had been nagging at me in my research was that I had very little understanding of the final days of William Alexander, the person I believed was ultimately responsible for the Oak Island mystery.

I hoped that maybe I'd find my answer here.

I asked the clerk if there were any books in her store from the 1600s. She laughed and said that everything in that area started in the 18th century. Instead, she said she'd show me the section on local history books.

As I followed her to that section and turned to go down the aisle I noticed a book on the bottom shelf just opposite the books she was leading me to.

The book had dull, illegible words on the spine and was packed in tightly with several other books. And yet, in my mind, it stood out.

As I turned to view the local history books it was like everything was a blur. I turned back to the book I'd seen and, pointing to the nondescript volume just behind us, I asked, "What is that book right there?"

She had no idea what it was, so I picked it up and started leafing through the pages. Lo and behold, there was an article in the book of over 100 pages in length that helped explain what happened to William Alexander at the end of his eventful life! That's the kind of thing that has happened to me, or for me, over the last seven years of involvement with this mystery of Oak Island.

With Oak Island we have legends of three secret societies possibly involved – the Knights Templar, the Freemasons and the Rosicrucians. I've added the history of a not-so-secret organization to the mix – the Knights Baronet of Nova Scotia – which, while not discreet in most of their actions, were definitely involved in clandestine activities in Nova Scotia. Also in this book, I am introducing an even lesser-known organization that may have played a role in the Oak Island story.

In the face of tales about a curse that haunts Oak Island, one thing I hope to show with this book, *Oak Island: Curses, Codes & Secret Societies*, is that there may be a way of understanding the island's history from an unorthodox point of view. Hopefully, this foray into strange stories and amazing facts will be enjoyable for you, the reader. If not, please don't put a curse on me!

Chapter One

THE ANATOMY OF A CURSE

A curse is typically thought of as an intention or expressed wish that misfortune might befall one or more people and, in some cases, even a place, for example Oak Island. In particular, a curse may refer to such a wish or idea to be carried out by a supernatural or spiritual power such as a god or devil, a spirit, a natural force or even as a kind of spell cast through magic or witchcraft. The curse and its ritual are assumed to play a role in the resulting bad luck of its intended victim.

Many a poor soul has been advised by a fortune teller that they have a curse on them and then are asked to pay even more money to have the curse removed. The act of reversing or eliminating a curse is, at times, called a removal or a breaking of the spell, and this requires its own elaborate rituals or prayers. In the old days this was called a "blunting" of the curse.

One method of reversing a curse was to bury an object upside down to confuse evil spirits. Even today, small religious statues are often buried upside down to blunt a curse or even to help sell a house. I've wondered why the 90' Stone found in the Oak Island Money Pit was buried with its message upside down. Perhaps it was for this very purpose of blunting an existing curse.

Whether you believe in curses or not, it has to be said that many curses, perhaps millions of curses, have been placed on people or places over many centuries.

Evidence of the curse exists in several proven forms from many cultures, which we'll take a quick look at.

The deliberate attempt to levy a curse is often part of the practice of magic and the study of various types of curses goes hand-in-hand with the study of both folk religion and folklore as far back as ancient India, Egypt, Israel, Africa, Greece and the Celtic/Roman Empires.

Since part of the success of at least some curses depends on the cursed person believing in the power of the hex, this can make that person hesitant, unsure and self-conscious to the point of losing their confidence, allowing bad things to happen inadvertently.

A curse can also be a convenient excuse to explain away naturally or accidently occurring incidents of unexplained human or equipment failure – the types of things that happen everywhere, curse or no curse.

As we know, curses often accompany tales of buried treasure. On May 23, 1701, at the execution dock at Wapping Old Stairs in London, England, a noose was placed around the neck of a pirate condemned to death for his wayward ways. The trapdoor snapped open and the doomed man dropped... all the way to the ground, with the rope snapped round his neck. Embarrassed, his executioners hoisted him a second time. This time the rope held and the notorious scourge of the seas, Captain William Kidd, was dead. But before he was captured it is said that he buried his treasure and cursed it.

It is well documented that before being taken into custody in Boston in 1699, Kidd buried treasure on Gardiners Island that was later dug up to be used as evidence against him. Theories abound regarding other places Kidd might have secreted valuables, from remote Japanese islands to other New England islands and, of course, on Oak Island.

One of those New England islands was Charles Island, named for King Charles I by its owner, Robert Gordon, William Alexander's premier Knight Baronet of Nova Scotia at the time. According to local legend, it was here that Kidd buried part of his secret booty – the treasure he had hoped to return for. To protect his stash, the pirate put a curse on the valuables and on anyone who might discover them.

However, the island Kidd chose was actually already cursed. Known by the nickname "The Thrice Cursed Island," Charles Island supposedly holds more than its fair share of bad luck. Originally cursed by a native chieftain who traded it away to European settlers, then again by Kidd to protect his treasure, it is said to have been cursed a third time when an unlucky local treasure hunter buried a different stash of cursed Aztec goods, transferring that bad luck to the island.

As with Oak Island, to this day no one has been known to have dug up the pirate treasure or the other cursed booty on Charles Island. What this highlights is that the story of a treasure buried on a cursed island is not unique to Oak Island, and may have been a symptom of the times.

There is no evidence that Captain Kidd ever visited Oak Island. Past owner and treasure hunter Gilbert Hedden was convinced that Kidd had nothing to do with a deposit of wealth on Oak Island but, instead, may have heard the same rumor others had heard.

In 1855, a few short newspaper articles were published in the *Portland* (Maine) *Advertiser* and other nearby newspapers about an island where treasure actually was found. One newspaper article reads:

> The **Portland Advertiser** *says that on Tuesday, while workmen of Dr. John Cummings, of Richmond's Island, were ploughing on the westerly side of the island, they turned up a pot containing seventeen gold coins of Charles II's time (along with) several pieces of silver and a gold ring. The coins bore upon one side the following inscription and device: In the centre, head of Charles II, with XX, surrounded by the words "CAROLUS D.G. MAG BR. FR. et HIB. REX." and "FLORENT CONCORDIA REGNA."*
>
> *The gold coin was as bright as though just from the mint. By whom it was deposited remains a mystery. Richmond's Island was one of the earliest spots settled in Maine and contained quite a large population for its time.*
>
> *The **Argus** (newspaper) says that upon the outside of the ring were the letters "G.V." and on the inner surface, the words "United Heartes death only partes."*

Can you imagine a similar pot being discovered on Oak Island during the current dig?

Another newspaper wrote:

CURIOUS DISCOVERY – While some workmen were digging in a field on Richmond's Island, in Casco Bay, a day or two since, they turned up a jar containing gold and silver coins. There were seventeen of the gold coins, of the denomination of £1 each and bore dates of James I and Charles I.

It is supposed that they were buried by some early inhabitants during some of the French or Indian difficulties, at the commencement of the settlement, that being one of the first spots settled in that vicinity.

Oddly, one newspaper states the coins had the dates of King Charles II, while another gives the dates of King James I and his son Charles I for the same coins!

Obviously, it would make a substantial difference if these coins bore dates of James I and Charles I, rather than Charles II, as this set of father and son kings are integral to my Oak Island theory.

It's no secret by now that my pet theory about Oak Island is that two men, William Alexander and Alexander Strachan, conspired to take a huge stolen Scottish treasure to Nova Scotia to finance a new colony. These men and their fellow Knights Baronet of Nova Scotia were supported in the endeavor by James I and his son Charles I. Some of their settlers escaped to Maine when France chased these Scots out of Nova Scotia.

As I've pointed out in my previous books, William Alexander was Earl of Stirling, Scotland, and the Strachan family was from Aberdeen, Scotland.

Captain William Kidd was born and raised almost dead center between these two places just one generation after the events in my theory took place.

Back in the 1930s Gilbert Hedden wrote to Franklin Roosevelt to say that he felt the Money Pit could have been created as early as 1635, for which I felt a certain satisfaction since my target date for Alexander's men to have buried something on Oak Island is 1632.

In 1967, in a letter to an Oak Island enthusiast named Robert Gay, Hedden writes: "I date the original work at about 1630 and I am convinced that the engineer who made the original layout had no intention of making a recovery in his lifetime but intended to leave it for future generations. I can also add that the original work was not too complicated and that I could duplicate it on the other end of the island in one summer season of work with no more that fifty men and using the same tools then available."

He also states: "I am very sure that Captain Kidd had nothing to do with the construction on Oak Island, but I do believe that he learned of it and gambled his life, or offered to, for an attempt to find it."

Hedden had spent a long time in England chasing down Captain Kidd's history, and further remarks: "My only conclusion is that Kidd, in his wanderings, learned of a very valuable cache, but he was uncertain as to its exact location or description."

I couldn't let this lie and began looking into whether there was any way Captain Kidd could have known about the Strachan/Alexander treasure. *Yes there was!*

Kidd is usually said to have been born in the town of Dundee, Scotland, in 1654. Some have said that it was Greenock, Scotland, but there is no proof of that. His father was John Kyd, a sailor who was lost at sea.

Dundee is situated almost exactly half-way between Stirling, Scotland, and Aberdeen, Scotland, roughly 60 miles in each direction. This is very significant.

An Alexander Kyd held land in Aberdeen in 1492. By 1520, the Kyd family began being recorded in the nearby town of Dundee, and continues to be up to this current day, spelled as both Kyd and Kidd.

In 1530, Alexander Kyd, possibly the one mentioned above, was the canon or high priest connected to the cathedral at Stirling, Scotland. William Alexander was the Earl of Stirling, and his family had lived near Stirling for at least a hundred years before William Kidd was even born. They would have lived there during the time that Alexander Kyd was the special or high priest at the Stirling Cathedral.

I believe a good part of the treasure hidden on Oak Island was from a treasure stolen by Al Strachan, partner to William Alexander. In October 1622, Strachan robbed George Keith, Earl Marischal (Marshal or top law officer of Scotland) of his fortune, reportedly unmatched by any other person in Scotland at the time.

As I explained in considerable detail in my *Oak Island Knights* book, Strachan's trial was delayed twice, and he eventually received a full pardon from the king. He was to be tried before the Privy Council, and William Alexander was a major leader of the Privy Council.

Oak Island: Curses, Codes & Secret Societies

Evidence seems to show that Strachan was pardoned in a high level conspiracy, leading him to become a partner to William Alexander, to being named a Knight Baronet and to donating at least a share of his ill-gotten plunder to help finance Nova Scotia.

There are many instances showing William Alexander lamenting about not being able to raise enough funds for his venture. This may have led him to take the drastic action of joining up with a known thief.

Strachan was pardoned in 1625. In that same year Alexander began the Knights Baronet of Nova Scotia. Al Strachan was part of a commission to recruit Baronets and signed a letter to help finance one of Alexander's ships. So we know he was deeply involved.

The Strachan family lived in Aberdeen all the way up to the time that at least three Strachan brothers moved to Halifax, Nova Scotia, located about an hour's drive from Oak Island. The Strachan name is still common in Aberdeen today. It is also common around Halifax.

The kicker is that, from 1841 until 1857, a man named John Strachan owned what are now known as the Nolan Cross lots on Oak Island. This was during the search activities of the Truro Company, with help from John Smith and Anthony Vaughan, two of the original diggers of the Money Pit (from back in 1795). They were, at the time of the Truro dig, in their seventies.

Dundee, Scotland, birthplace of Captain Kidd, is also located only about forty miles from Benholm Castle, whose title deed was mentioned specifically in a list of the treasure stolen by Alexander Strachan.

The current Strachan family owners of Benholm Castle discovered a secret tunnel that led a distance away from the castle, which local legend says was used by smugglers and possibly involved monks.

Perhaps related to this story, a church in Storrington, England, received pews made of wood from Nova Scotia in commemoration of the role they played in spiriting wealth to Nova Scotia for "safekeeping." This came from an email forwarded to me by the Oak Island team, sent to them by the church historian. This church is also connected to a specific Knight Baronet of Nova Scotia.

One scenario could be that the treasure Strachan stole was smuggled out of Benholm Castle through the secret tunnel and taken to the nearby sea coast. From there it may have been taken by ship to Storrington where it was hidden by monks until William Alexander's ships sailed to Nova Scotia with it. Alexander's flagship, the *Eagle*, was anchored in the Thames River, basically just around the corner from Storrington.

The records of the fleet's voyage say that, just before the trip began, the ships were gathered together at the Dunes, which is a safe harbor along the coast of the English Channel not far from Storrington.

All of this needs further research but does present an enticing answer as to how and from where the Strachan treasure made its way to ships bound for Nova Scotia.

One interesting point to be added here is that William Alexander received a "safe passage" letter from the king for his four ships. This letter obviously would do him no good once they left the English coastline.

No French or Spanish ship was going to honor it, and there was no appreciable British presence in Nova Scotia at the time. But this letter would have been of great value if a stop was to be made near Storrington to load a secret cargo bound for Nova Scotia.

In an area so small as to include Aberdeen, Benholm Castle, Dundee and Stirling, it is likely that just about everyone living nearby would have heard of this major robbery of the Earl Marischal of Scotland, possibly the richest, and certainly one of the most powerful men in all of Scotland. The fact that Keith's wife, 30 years his junior, was also stolen makes this an even more scandalous crime for that time and location.

Imagine that in the region in which you live someone steals a massive treasure and the younger wife of one of the most powerful men around and gets away with it literally "Scot free." It is likely that you and everyone around you would know of it and that the story might be told for generations to come – even told to a young William Kidd.

If Hedden is correct, it is entirely possible that William Kidd heard of the Strachan treasure, stolen only a generation before his birth, and also of the Nova Scotia adventure led by William Alexander, the Earl of nearby Stirling – a town where Kidd's ancestor, or at least a forefather, once served as the high priest.

I've said for a long time that I think a few families knew a lot about the treasure, and a lot of families knew a little about the treasure. And it can be safely concluded that the idea of cursing a buried treasure is very real.

It is quite likely that Captain Kidd learned of a cursed treasure buried somewhere in Nova Scotia, considering where he was born and raised.

This brings me to some recent research I've done on curses in the form of "curse tablets."

Cultures around the world have had their own set of curse practices, the curse tablet being one of the more commonly used tools. This research may present a fresh explanation for the so-called "Oak Island 90′ Stone."

The modern practice of throwing coins into springs, fountains and wells continues a very ancient tradition, one that has survived into recent times particularly in the form of wishing wells. This is especially true in those parts of Europe which have a Celtic connection. Such was the opinion of Romans who recorded that the Celts were renowned for their fascination with springs, rivers and lakes, and for their offerings at these locations.

This is thought to be based on the contemplative nature of deep pools and the therapeutic powers of natural springs. Celts would throw in coins, jewelry or other personal possessions, and also curse tablets as offerings to *Aquae Sulis* (goddess of water), as represented today, in Bath, England, at the ancient Roman Baths.

Aquae Sulis is a natural mineral spring found in the valley of the Avon River in Southwest England. It is the only spring in Britain officially designated as "hot." The name is Latin for "the waters of Sulis."

The Romans purposely identified the Celtic goddess Sulis with their goddess Minerva, and encouraged her worship. Thus the spring was named for her.

The similarities between Minerva and Sulis helped the Celts adapt to Roman culture, and the spring was built into a major Roman bath complex associated with an adjoining temple.

About 130 messages to Sulis scratched onto lead curse tablets have been recovered from the sacred spring by archaeologists. This collection is the most important found in Britain. Most of the tablets were written in Latin, although some of those discovered were in a Brythonic language. Those who wrote the tablets usually laid curses upon others they felt had done them wrong.

It should also be noted that a hoard of 30,000 silver coins, one of the largest discovered in Britain, was unearthed in an archaeological dig in 2012. The coins, believed to date from the 3rd century, were found not far from the Roman baths.

What if this would happen on Oak Island?!

Curse tablets were often thrown in water or buried underground to invoke a curse against someone who had done another person wrong, hoping to have something horrible happen to that person. Many curse tablets have been found buried in what were once Celtic areas. This practice may have been adopted from the Romans who dominated the Celts for centuries.

Early Greco-Roman curses are typically those of a conditional type, inscribed on armor or weapons, such as: "Whoever steals this, may he be accursed." These expressions are different from the more complex tradition of magical, evil curses, but some did call on evil spirits or, alternatively, on holy beings or on God for help.

Motives for early curses generally involved obtaining revenge against a thief, or to ask for protection of valuables. These tablets sometimes sought to recover items like clothing, jewelry and/or various amounts of money. However, the original practice of threatening with a curse changed over time to an outright curse against a perceived enemy or competitor.

Egypt has also been the source of a number of discovered curse tablets. Shown (at right) is an Egyptian stone with a carved curse inscription. This tablet is made of limestone and appears to date to roughly the 3rd Intermediate Period of Egypt, probably from 825-773 BCE.

Found buried underground in Mendes, Egypt, this stone depicts the high priest and the prince of Mendes. The carved stone tablet celebrates a donation of land for an Egyptian temple and places a curse on anyone who would misappropriate the land.

It's not hard to jump from this symbol-carved Egyptian curse stone to the strange symbols carved on the *Close-up of Egyptian carving.* stone found at the 90' level of the apparently cursed Oak Island Money Pit. For those who might think this idea is too bizarre, keep in mind how bizarre it would be to place instructions on how to dig up the pit at the bottom of the pit. That makes absolutely no sense at all!

Coincidentally, the foundation for at least one of our three secret societies from Oak Island legend also begins with stonemasons in Egypt. It was here that secrets in the form of construction techniques began to be developed and then to be held within a tight group of guild workers for many centuries, who thus benefitted financially from using this exclusive information.

Later, stonemason guilds and lodges throughout medieval history built some of the most magnificent man-made structures in the world. During at least a few centuries, from 1119 to their disbandment in 1312, the Knights Templar worked very closely with stonemason lodges as financiers of magnificent buildings, some of which still stand, and are being used today as churches and centers of learning or exploration.

This is one of the simplest explanations for a link between the Knights Templar and the Freemasons, who eventually arose from ranks of operative stonemasons. However, that link may have been made specifically possible through the Knights Baronet of Nova Scotia, as I will soon explain.

While the Egyptian example was cut in stone, the curse tablet was often made of etched or scribed metal which was then buried in the ground. Tablets were used to ask various gods and other powers, even the deceased, to perform an action on a person or object, or otherwise affect the subject of the curse, much like the supposed "Curse of Oak Island" does. Stone tablets were typically placed upside down underground, either buried in graves or tombs, or even thrown into wells or pools.

Sometimes they were placed in an underground sanctuary and, if made of metal, nailed to the walls of temples. They were also used for love spells. When employed in this manner they were placed inside the home of the desired target of affection.

Tablets are sometimes discovered along with small dolls or figurines (at times inaccurately referred to as Voodoo dolls) which may also be pierced by nails. These figurines attempted to resemble the love subject and often had both their feet and hands bound. Curse tablets might also have hair or pieces of clothing attached.

Not all tablets found included a personal name. It is clear, especially in the Roman period, that tablets were sometimes prepared in advance, with space left for inserting the names provided by a paying customer.

People in many ancient societies believed they could use magic to control the natural world. All levels of society, regardless of economic or class status, believed in such magic, even kings and queens.

There have been roughly 1600 curse tablets discovered, mostly written in Greek. Of these Greek tablets, 220 were located near Athens, Greece. However, the first set of curse tablets to be discovered came from the city of Selinus, in Sicily, part of the Roman Empire. In this case, a total of twenty-two tablets were found, mostly coming from the early 5th century, and directed toward someone that the user was apparently suing.

One possibility is that the idea of a stone or piece of metal being buried or kept with a valuable item was brought to the British Isles by Roman conquerors.

Discovery of the oldest ever curse tablet, dating to 3,200 BCE, was just announced in March 2022, during the final writing of *Oak Island Curses, Codes and Secret Societies*. Found in the West Bank region between Israel and Jordan, the first line reads: "Cursed, cursed, cursed by the God YHW" (a Hebrew symbol for God).

While the ancient Israelites, Greeks and Romans may have feared the power of these tablets, some historians have argued that they were produced in a fit of anger or envy towards an enemy or athletic opponent. Others are viewed as self-imposed contracts to accept both the blessings and the curses that might come along with acquiring land or other valuable possessions.

Despite their many superstitions, modern athletes have nothing on the athletes of old who wrote some incredibly evil curses on tablets that have been found buried in the old Roman Empire. Four are shown here:

•*I adjure you, demon whoever you are, and I demand of you from this hour, from this day, from this moment that you torture and kill the horses of the Greens and Whites and that you kill in a crash their drivers…and leave not a breath in their bodies;*

•*Help me in the circus on 8 November. Bind every limb, every sinew, the shoulders, the ankles and the elbows of Olympus, Olympianus, Scortius and Juvencus, the charioteers of the Red. Torment their minds, their intelligence and their senses so that they may not know what they are doing, and knock out their eyes so that they may not see where they are going—neither they nor the horses they are going to drive;*

•*Bind the horses whose names and images are on this implement. Bind their running, their power, their soul, their onrush, their speed. Take away their victory, entangle their feet, hinder them, hobble them so that tomorrow morning in the hippodrome they are not able to run or walk about or win or go out of the starting gates or advance on the racecourse or track, but may they fall down with their drivers;*

•*I conjure you up, holy beings and holy names, join in aiding this spell and bind, enchant, thwart, strike, overturn, conspire against, destroy, kill, break Eucherius, the charioteer, and all his horses tomorrow in the circus at Rome. May he not leave the barriers well; may he not be quick in contest; may he not outstrip anyone; may he not make the turns well; may he not win any prize.*

While requests were being made of a wide variety of supernatural entities, note that the last example appeals to "holy beings" for help. This tablet and the recently announced West Bank tablet, which also calls on God for help, may together be significant in understanding the 90′ Stone found in the Money Pit. The ultimate chiseled stones carrying the name of God, I suppose, would be the *Ten Commandments*, which presumably lie buried with the Ark of the Covenant somewhere in the world.

The idea of curse tablets somehow made its way into Celtic society as well, and it may have made its way to Oak Island via the Scots who settled in Nova Scotia from 1623 through 1632, if it can be shown that the so-called 90′ Stone also calls on God for assistance, rather than representing instructions on how to retrieve a treasure.

The Bath curse tablets are a collection of about 130 Roman era tablets discovered in 1979/1980, in the English city of Bath. Some of these tablets invoke the intercession of the goddess Sulis or Minerva in the return of stolen goods, as they curse the perpetrators of the thefts. They represent another set of examples where a so-called curse tablet is buried which asks for the intercession of God, of a goddess, or of holy beings and holy names, showing this to be a common occurrence.

These people would have been a healthy combination of Romans, Celts, Brits and likely even Picts – people who had been conquered or driven together by the expanding Roman Empire.

Most of the inscriptions are in colloquial Latin, known as "British Latin." However, some of the inscriptions are in a language which is not Latin, although they use Roman lettering. They may be in a British Celtic language not yet totally understood.

Shown in the photo at right is one of the many curse tablets found at Bath. It reads: "May he who carried off Vilbia from me become liquid as the water. May he who so obscenely devoured her become dumb."

Yet another curse tablet shown below, also found at Bath, England, and translated by the British Museum, reads: "I curse Tretia Maria and her life and mind and memory and liver and lungs mixed up together, and her words, thoughts and memory; thus may she be unable to speak what things are concealed."

If these tablets remind you of the many stone carvings found on Oak Island, it may not be all that coincidental. It's tempting to wonder – could the stone found in the Money Pit, buried upside down, at approximately 90 feet, actually have been a curse tablet or blessing request aimed at protecting the treasure hidden there, or blunting its curse? – a tablet that also calls on God for help?

On the following page is shown author Edward Snow's drawing from 1949 of what he was told the Oak Island stone, found in 1804, looked like. There have been a handful of translations of this code and you are about to hear of a new one.

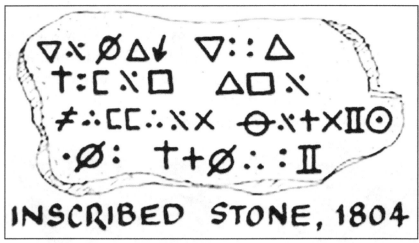

Another commonly referred to stone found on Oak Island is the so-called "H.O. Stone" (shown below), which was discovered by Gilbert Hedden, in 1936, at Joudrey's Cove.

Oddly, among the long list of valuable items of the Strachan treasure, part of which I believe may have been buried on Oak Island, is the item: "ane jasp stone for steming of bluid" (or a healing stone). In this case, even possibly the richest man in all of Scotland seemed to still believe in magic stones. So did Mary, Queen of Scots.

Later in this book I will tell how she fits in.

Whether in stone or in metal, curse tablets were usually deposited where it was thought the gods or demons could read them. Eventually, verbal curses, at least in the most extreme cases, captured public attention and the curse tablet was left for archeologists to discover, just like the stone tablets and markers on Oak Island.

Verbal curses often accompanied someone who was being executed, as in the case of witches, and even in the case of the famous Knights Templar curse of Jacques de Molay (last known leader of this organization), which was placed on a French king and a Roman pope. Molay is credited with being the very last of the Grand Masters of the original Knights Templar, leading the Order from April 20, 1292, until it was dissolved by the command of Pope Clement V in 1312.

It has been claimed that Molay cursed King Philip IV of France and his descendants from his own execution pyre. This story was told by a contemporary writer, Ferretto of Vicenza. The lead Knights Templar was brought before Pope Clement V, whom he denounced for his injustice. Later, as he was about to be executed, Molay appealed "from this your heinous judgement to the living and true God, who is in Heaven."

Molay warned the pope that, within a year and a day, he and King Philip IV would be obliged to answer for their crimes in God's presence.

King Philip and Pope Clement both died within a year of Molay's execution; Clement succumbed to a long illness on April 20, 1314, and Philip died due to a stroke while hunting.

Then followed in rapid succession, between 1314 and 1328, the deaths of the last direct Capetian kings of France – the three sons and a grandson of Philip IV.

Within fourteen years of the death of Molay, the 300-year-old House of Capet collapsed. American historian Henry Charles Lea wrote: "Even in distant Germany, King Philip's death was spoken of as a retribution for his destruction of the Templars, and Clement was described as shedding tears of remorse on his deathbed for the ruin of the Templars."

Some curses stand out as undying legends, especially the curse that was apparently placed on the Oak Island Money Pit, in Nova Scotia, though no one seems to know who was behind it... or do we?

We do know that many of the "origin stories" of the Oak Island treasure emanate from Scotland in one form or another. For example, we have the escaping Knights Templars, Sir Henry Sinclair's North Atlantic travels, and my pet theory concerning Sir William Alexander, founder of Nova Scotia, and his partner Al Strachan, the known thief of a large treasure. Some of this treasure may have ended up on Oak Island, and with it carried its own special curse, long before reaching Nova Scotia.

Chapter Two

THE CURSE OF OAK ISLAND

Since the story of the so-called "Curse of Oak Island" is what prompted this book, it would only be fitting to dig into that tale right now.

A quick explanation of Oak Island generally involves the story that, in 1795, three young men discovered a depression in the ground on an island located in Mahone Bay, along the Atlantic coastline of Nova Scotia. In this bay are several islands (around 365). Oak Island stands out as the only one with a curse attached.

The hunt for treasure on Oak Island has persisted ever since the depression was first found, at least according to legend. The date 1795 comes from legend more so than from written records. There is some evidence of this date being correct to be found in the fact that John Smith, one of the discoverers of the Money Pit depression, purchased the lot that contained it, also in 1795.

The exact beginnings of the treasure hunt may be somewhat clouded, but it is true that the idea of a curse being connected to this search is real, whether the curse is real or not. The basic curse says that six people have died actively trying to recover the treasure and that a seventh person engaged in physically searching for it must die in order for the treasure to be found.

One version of the curse says that when the last oak tree dies, the treasure will be found. This apparently was never an actual curse.

In 1934, a newspaperman was simply writing about the Oak Island oak trees: "Fifty years ago, old Chester people remember, there was a regular little grove of these live-oaks on the spit at Smith's Cove. Most of them have died. Now a mere half dozen hoary and moribund old-timers remain with a kind of struggling majesty. I would like to say that there is a legend that when the last live-oak dies, the island will yield the secret of its treasure, but I heard of no such legend. It seems a pity." (By the way, Chester is a town across the bay from Oak Island).

These words were written by Frederick Griffin in an article which appeared in the October 13, 1934 issue of the *Toronto Star Weekly*, a Canadian periodical published from 1910 until 1973. Griffin was merely musing about all the stories told about Oak Island. He made this off-hand remark, which was then picked up as some kind of old curse. It never was one because it never existed until he wrote the above quote.

The "seven must die," curse also appears to have come from an off-hand remark to a journalist.

Research done by Doug Crowell, one of the top Oak Island historians alive today, came up with a list of fourteen people who are known to have passed away on Oak Island. Of course, many other people who once worked on Oak Island digs, likely numbering in the hundreds by now, have also died, particularly two long-time Oak Islanders, Fred Nolan and Dan Blankenship.

Doug's list is simply documenting the fourteen people known to have died on Oak Island and not all of them were engaged specifically in digging for treasure at the time that they passed away. They are:

- Thomas Duncan Smith - son of John Smith, died February 19, 1803;
- William Smith - son of John Smith, died August 2, 1830;
- John Smith - son of John Smith, died of Scarlet Fever on February 27, 1837;
- James Smith, died by accident, but not known to be digging for treasure at the time;
- Ann - wife of John Smith, died December 19, 1852;
- Rachel Smith - daughter of John Smith, died April 5, 1854;
- John Smith, died September 29 1857;
- Unknown worker, died in a boiler explosion, 1861;
- Maynard Kaiser, died March 26, 1897, in a fall down a shaft;
- John W. MacGinnis - descendant of Donald Daniel McInnis (the spelling of this name varied), and an Oak Island resident, died February 4, 1939;
- Robert Restall Senior, died August 17, 1965;
- Robert Restall Junior, died August 17, 1965;
- Cyril Hiltz, died August 17, 1965;
- Carl Graeser, died August 17, 1965.

The last four men died on the same day in what has become known as the Restall Tragedy. The other two that make up the "six men have died" part of the curse were the unknown worker and Maynard Kaiser.

Of the non-searching deaths, the Smith family makes up all but one. Based on the ages of the deceased it seems that life on Oak Island must have been tough at times.

In 1965, the Restall family work crew experienced the worst loss of life of any of the Oak Island expeditions when Robert Restall Sr. looked down a shaft he had been working on the day before and was overcome by some type of poisonous fumes. His son Robert Jr. went to his rescue and was also overcome. The same fate befell two Restall workers, Cyril Hiltz and Carl Graeser.

It is often stated that seven must die before the treasure is found, but that they must die while actively searching for the treasure. Oddly enough, none of these four men were actively searching for treasure that day. Robert Sr. was heading into town and just casually thought, before leaving, that he'd take a look down the shaft he'd been working on the previous day. He was suddenly overcome by some type of gas. The other three men who died were trying to save his life, not searching for treasure.

It may be just a matter of semantics. Others who have died, especially Fred Nolan and Dan Blankenship, had never given up their interest in the treasure hunt and were working with the current team, on and off, at the times of their deaths, although neither passed away while on Oak Island or while physically seeking treasure.

Beyond all this confusion about the curse there are indications from a couple of old newspaper articles that three additional diggers perished when a shaft they were digging quickly filled with water while they were down about 100 feet. This seems to bring the total to nine.

The actual wording of the article states: "Once, in the late 1890s, three workmen were trapped and killed when part of the tunnel collapsed."

If this is true, and I've seen another similar news article, then we actually have nine men that were killed "actively searching" for treasure on Oak Island, not the six typically reported.

A discovery was made that the origin of the "seven must die" curse may have been another misquoting or misinterpretation of a comment made by the bereaved girlfriend of one of those who died in the Restall accident. It is said that she made an off -hand comment something to the effect that, "Is it going to take seven people dying before they quit looking for treasure on that cursed island?"

This comment was picked up and published in 1967 as the "seven must die curse." It appeared in the January 1967 issue of *True: The Man's Magazine*, with a front page headline – "Tantalizing Treasure: Oak Island's Death-Filled Search Continues."

This is the first known mention of the curse and it was based on a grieving girlfriend's mournful response.

True actually featured Oak Island in an article just ten years earlier, in September 1957. The front page splash for this article read: "Strange Story Of The Mysterious Money Pit." In that "strange story," no mention was made of the "seven must die" curse. So it seems that this oft-repeated curse was a figment of the imagination of the *True* reporter who traveled to Nova Scotia to report on the 1965 Restall accident two years later.

The 1965 *Reader's Digest* article that has inspired so many people to spend their lives and fortunes searching for treasure on Oak Island never once mentioned this curse, even though it is typically presented as a well-known, long-time curse concerning the island.

The famous June 2, 1862, letter by searcher Jotham McCully talks about the three men who first found the Money Pit trying to get help from nearby Chester.

McCully states: "By this time the work became too heavy for them to carry on alone, and they tried to get the inhabitants to join them; but they refused from a kind of superstitious dread." This is the first printed mention of an Oak Island superstition, but not a curse.

There is also the tale of a superstition that supposedly began in 1720. Two men rowed out to the island to investigate some lights they had seen, and never returned. However, there is not enough available evidence to prove that there was any substantial number of people even living near Oak Island in 1720.

An article appeared in the *Riverside Daily Press*, Riverside, California, on July 10, 1926. In the retelling of the discovery of the Money Pit, the author states that there was little interest in going to the island to see what the three young men had found because: "It was haunted, they said, with every sort of horrid apparition. It emitted sulphurous fires at night and rang with groans and shrieks of the hair-raising kind."

In saying all of this, my theory about the treasure at least partially buried on Oak Island involves another curse which seems to have come true.

In the early 1600s, George Keith was the Earl Marischal (or the Marshal) of Scotland, basically the chief law enforcement officer. His family had held this position for several generations and was able to build up a massive amount of wealth, which was stolen in October 1622.

In fact, in a few of my Oak Island books I reprinted the complete stolen treasure list as presented at court against the perpetrators. It took up about half the page size as the one you are currently reading. It appears the treasure could now be worth as much as a billion U.S. dollars.

To put the enormity of this in perspective, just one single item on the Keith/Strachan stolen treasure list consisted of "16,000 merks of silver and gold ready for coinage." According to a contemporary reference, 3,000 merks equaled 150 to 160 British pounds. Using just the smaller worth of 150 pounds, 16,000 merks would then equal 800 British pounds in 1622, the year it was stolen.

The following is from a currency conversion chart:

If you want to compare the value of £800 Income or Wealth, in 1622, there are four choices (to convert to the U.S. dollar). *In 2021, the relative value of...*
- *Real wage or real wealth value of that income or wealth is $199,187;*
- *Labor earnings of that income or wealth is $3,363,800;*
- *Relative income value of that income or wealth is $6,100,710;*
- *Relative output value of that income or wealth is $66,747,800.*

That is potentially over $66 million for just this one item, and this wasn't even the largest item on the list!

The very first item on the stolen treasure list consisted of 26,000 pounds (assuming British pounds sterling, not in weight) in "Portuguese ducats and other species."

What is very interesting is that, during the 2021 dig season on Oak Island, the team found gold thought to be of Portuguese origin that somehow rubbed on to pieces of iron. In 1654, an "iron box" belonging to James Keith, son of Al Strachan's robbery victim, George Keith, was located on the Orkney Islands just off the north coast of Scotland. With several witnesses on hand the treasure chest was pried open. Inside was found a small number of items that seemed as though they matched closely to some items found on the original robbery list.

The key here is that the treasure chest is described as an iron box. If the scraps of metal found on Oak Island were from a similar iron box that instead held 26,000 British pounds worth of Portuguese ducats, and that iron box had since decayed or had been destroyed through treasure hunting, this would explain how Portuguese gold could be found rubbed against iron. I'll have more on the Portuguese connection possibly in a future book.

Meanwhile, the relative value of these ducats?

- *Real wage or real wealth value of that income or wealth is $6,474,620;*
- *Labour earnings of that income or wealth is $109,309,600;*
- *Relative income value of that income or wealth is $198,353,000;*
- *Relative output value of that income or wealth is $2,169,790,000.*

That last number is 2+ BILLION dollars!

The four choices of valuation show just how difficult it is to put an exact figure on the worth of this treasure. Using the highest rate, these two items together would be worth over 3.7 BILLION dollars in "output value." Their "relative income value" would equal $341,053,000.

If the writers of the treasure list actually meant 26,000 pounds of Portuguese ducats in weight, 16 ounces to the pound would mean 16 x 26,000 or 416,000 ounces of gold. Gold, as of this writing, is worth $1,954 per ounce so 416,000 ounces times $1,954 per ounce equals a whopping $812,864,000 just in Portuguese coins.

These are only two of the items on the treasure list out of about 20 or more listed. Other researchers have estimated the total treasure to be worth over $4 billion current U.S. dollars and no one seems to know what happened to it unless maybe the Oak Island team is still searching for it right now, curse and all.

The owner of this treasure, Earl George Keith, was married twice, both times to a woman named Margaret. His first wife was Margaret Home, the only daughter of Alexander Home, 5th Lord Home. This Margaret passed away in 1598, but not without first dreaming of a curse that would befall her husband, destroying the vast fortune he amassed, inherited or had stolen. This curse concerned the Abbey of Deer. Yes, Deer Abbey!

For more than 300 years, Deer Abbey was home to Cistercian monks. They seem to have lived a quiet and contemplative life until the Protestant Reformation of 1560 brought the abbey's spiritual use to a close.

Cistercians had a close link to the Knights Templar. The abbey is also associated with the *Book of Deer* which was probably kept in its library. This gospel book was written around A.D. 900 but contains many additions from around 200 years later. These additions are the oldest body of Gaelic writings in Scotland.

In 1114, Hugues de Payens, co-founder of the Order of the Knights Templar, left for the Holy Land where, with eight other companions, he founded the Poor Knights of Christ, formed to protect pilgrims. On January 13, 1128, the Council of Troyes, under the leadership of Bernard de Clairvaux, ratified the Order of the Knights Templar.

The cult of the Order existed until the 14th century, and its legends have continued to play a huge role in many mysteries around the western world, whether the Templars were truly involved or not.

Two years earlier, in 1112, Bernard de Clairvaux entered the Cistercian Abbey of Cîteaux. The Cistercians might have remained a relatively small family had not the fortunes of the Order been changed by St. Bernard, who joined Cîteaux as a novice along with about 30 relatives and friends.

In 1115, Bernard was sent out as founding abbot of Clairvaux. The growth of the Order was spectacular. No other religious body was increased so greatly in so brief a time. Historians have concluded that St. Bernard de Clairvaux founded 76 monasteries spread throughout Europe: 35 in France, 14 in Spain, ten in England and Ireland, six in the Flanders area of Belgium, four in Italy, four in Denmark, two in Sweden and one in Hungary.

Other reports say that by 1151, two years before Bernard's death, there were 500 Cistercian abbeys, and that Clairvaux had 700 monks under his direction.

With large estates and a large disciplined, unpaid labor force the Cistercians were able to develop all branches of farming without the hindrance of costs and complexities faced by most farmers. In reclaiming marginal land and by increasing production, especially that of wool in the large pastures of Wales and Yorkshire, the Cistercians played a large role in the economic progress of the 12th century. They also contributed to the development of more modern techniques of farming.

The golden age for the Cistercians was the 12th century. Even before its close, however, many abbeys were breaking some of the most essential statutes by accumulating wealth through accepting feudal tenants and tithes, and by commercial transactions in wool and grain. They were also involved in gold mining.

In 1219, Deer Abbey was founded at a place called Deer, which had previously been an old Celtic monastery and which, according to tradition, was first founded by St. Columba, perhaps the most famous of the ancient Celtic monks. It is said that Columba put a curse on the land of the abbey, saying, "Whosoever should come against it, let him not be of many years, or victorious."

The monastery was, of course, of the Catholic religion. In 1543, Robert Keith, a forefather of Marischal George Keith, was appointed "commendam" or "commentator" of the abbey, a position in lieu of a priest being present to handle the finances and wealth generated there.

This was meant by the church to be a temporary position filled by a layman until such time as a new priest could be installed. The problem was that Scotland was undergoing great changes, especially in the replacement of the Catholic religion with the Presbyterian religion.

As long as the abbey had remained Catholic, and the amount of commercialism was kept reasonable (and used to support the church) it seems the spirit of St. Columba was satisfied. However, with the switch in religion, the Abbey of Deer was finally relinquished to King James VI (later James I), who created a temporal or secular lordship to oversee the lands of the old abbey, and this lordship fell upon the shoulders of Earl Marischal George Keith.

When George Keith accepted lordship of the lands of the abbey his first wife had a terrible dream as described by Patrick Gordon in *A Short Abridgement of Britane's Distemper, from the Yeares of God 1639 to 1649*, in which he writes:

> *This was a fearful presage of the fatal punishment which did hang over the head of that noble family by a terrible vision to his grandmother* (this being Margaret {Home} Keith, first wife of George Keith), *after the sacrilegious annexing of the Abbey of Deer to the house of Marshall, which I think not unworthy the remembrance, were it but to advise other noblemen thereby to beware of meddling with the rents of the Church, for in the first foundation thereof they were given out with a **curse** pronounced in their character: "Cursed be those that taketh this away from the holy use whereunto it is now dedicated."*

Patrick Gordon ends this story with a warning:

Meddle nae wi' holy things, for 'gin ye dee,
A weird, I rede, in some shape shall follow thee.

The word weird (late Middle English) originally meant something "having the power to control destiny." Translated, the above caution reads:

Meddle not with holy things, for when you do,
A power controlling your destiny, I read, in some
shape shall follow you.

The wealth of the Abbey of Deer, which made up a large percentage of George Keith's vast treasure, appears to have been the subject of a curse and a dire warning – the curse of St. Columba: "Whosoever should come against it, let him not be of many years, or victorious," otherwise written as: "Cursed be those that taketh this away from the holy use whereunto it is now dedicated," plus the admonition: "Meddle nae wi' holy things, for 'gin ye dee, a weird, I rede, in some shape shall follow thee."

Whether the curse was activated or it was just a strange coincidence, no one can argue that George Keith had his destiny controlled through the actions of Al Strachan. He lost everything he had, including his young wife, and he died shortly thereafter.

George Keith's son, William, joined with Al Strachan as a partner and fellow Knight Baronet of Nova Scotia, even though it was his own inheritance that Strachan had stolen.

George Keith's second wife, thirty years his junior, was Margaret Ogilvy, daughter of James, 5th Lord Ogilvy.

Whether Al Strachan fell in love with her or her money, the two were carrying on an affair during the last couple years of George Keith's life. Keith died April 2, 1623, with his wife and her lover under indictment.

Among the early partners of Sir William Alexander were Sir William Douglas, who was also charged in the Keith robbery, and Sir David Livingstone, who had acted as cautioner for Strachan's appearance in court. A cautioner is a person who assumes legal responsibility for the fulfillment of another's debt or obligation and himself becomes liable if the other defaults.

The final partner was Robert Gordon who handled special military/intelligence projects for both King James and King Charles. King James founded the Knights Baronet of Nova Scotia and King Charles chartered every one of them until his beheading in 1649. They included Strachan, Keith, Douglas, Livingstone and Gordon.

This cadre made up the initial partners of Sir William Alexander the Elder, and his son, Sir William Alexander the Younger, who was first in command in Nova Scotia, with George Home, the nephew of George Keith, as second in command. Home was also a Knight Baronet.

Keith's yearly income has been estimated to have been roughly 22,500 British pounds compared with the average English nobleman's income of just £3020, or anywhere from five million to one billion current U.S. dollars per year! It's not hard to imagine how his treasure and its curse might have been transported to Oak Island.

Chapter Three

THE "DIGGINS"

According to many Oak Island traditions, and to some contemporary writings, a stone with symbols on it was found at the bottom of the Money Pit in 1804 by workers who had reached between the 80 and 90 foot levels deep into the earth. It was lying upside down.

Some folks have questioned the stone's existence, or at least its relevance. However, there are reasons to believe the stone was real and that the code inscribed on it was passed down through the years, despite the stone disappearing somewhere along the way.

It is uncanny how certain aspects of the Oak Island story can get misconstrued and then repeated as gospel. For instance, the so-called 90' Stone has been said to have been found at 68 feet, 80 feet, 83 feet and at 90 feet.

I suppose we never will know the true depth.

Another example is that it is often stated that Daniel McGinnis, as a young lad, was drawn to the island by strange lights and accidentally found the Money Pit depression. And yet, one of the earliest records of the "Diggins" on Oak Island states that "Mr. McGinnis went to the island to make a farm." This rings true when compared to old land deeds and surveys showing lots that were purchased on the island before 1795.

This early story of Oak Island appeared in 1862, in an issue of the *Liverpool Transcript* newspaper, and earlier in the *Halifax Sun* newspaper. I bought a digital copy of the *Transcript* version from the Nova Scotia Archives so that I could read the "Oak Island Diggins" article firsthand.

It was written by J. B. or Jotham McCully although, like other misinterpretations, he did not request that the article be published in these newspapers. He actually wrote it as a letter to a man in Halifax who then took it to the *Halifax Sun*.

Even McCully's true name is confusing as it is also given as Jonathan Blanchard McCully and often confused with another Jonathan Blanchard McCully who lived in Nova Scotia around the same time.

Some skeptics argue with the idea that if all of what McCully wrote was true, why wasn't it written about years before – when it is said to have happened? My answer is that there were no newspapers in Nova Scotia for most of those early years. There was also no photography available to the common man until 1888, although tintype photography was around by the 1860s. And, most importantly, there doesn't appear to have been an actual Nova Scotia Historical Society at the time.

It is said that a man named John Hunter-Duvar was somehow involved in the history of Oak Island and that he was the secretary for the Nova Scotia Historical Society. This man was born John Hunter but, because there was another John Hunter on Prince Edward Island (where this man had a farm), he chose to add Duvar to his last name so that he would get the correct mail.

Hunter-Duvar was born in Newburgh, Scotland, and after 1850 was based in Halifax as a press agent for the Associated Press of New York. He was known to be living in Halifax, for sure, from 1863 through 1868. Hunter-Duvar may have (and I'm only speculating) actually been the very man to whom Jotham McCully originally sent the 1862 letter.

The first attempt to form a Historical Society of Nova Scotia took place in 1850 but failed, it is thought, because of "strong political feelings which at the time divided the people of the Capital," namely Halifax.

A second attempt "made by Mr. Hunter-Duvar, in 1863, met with a like fate, and it is supposed, from the same cause," according to Historical Society records.

Finally, on January 2, 1878, the Royal Nova Scotia Historical Society was fully formed and incorporated.

Hunter-Duvar is the only recorded member of the 1863 society that I have been able to find. So, a likely scenario is that he contacted McCully to get a story for the Associated Press, perhaps passing himself off as secretary of a fledgling Historical Society.

He also likely made a little money having McCully's letter published in both the *Liverpool Transcript* and *Halifax Sun* newspapers. Again, this is only my speculation.

Another simple reason the so-called "Diggins" on Oak Island were not widely known about might be the philosophy expressed to me by Nova Scotia sea captain and successful treasure hunter Captain Robert MacKinnon that "treasure hunters don't tell their secrets; otherwise they won't get the treasure."

As far as I can tell there is no reason to disbelieve what McCully wrote as his best understanding of the history of the Money Pit dig from 1795 through 1862. I repeat his entire letter here for your enjoyment, and will pick up my story on the other end –

Truro, June 2, 1862

Having been ridiculed both by the press and the uniformed portion of the public embarking in so foolish an enterprise as the "Oak Island Diggins," we propose giving to the public something in the shape of a reason for our great faith in that enterprise.

When the first settlers from the United States came to Chester, they brought with them a story that an old sailor, while on his death bed, stated that he belonged to Captain Kidd's crew, and that he helped to bury on an Island, somewhere in that neighborhood, about two millions pound value of treasure, but that he had never dared to avail himself of the secret for fear of the "law" taking hold of him as a Pirate.

Sometime after the arrival of these persons a Mr. McGinnis went to Oak Island to make a farm, when he discovered the spot in question from its being sunken, and from the position of three oak trees, which stood in a triangular form round the pit. The bark had letters cut into it with a knife on each tree facing the pit, and one of the trees being so directly over the pit, that two large branches formed a crotch, were exactly perpendicular to the centre, and had a hole bored through, and an oak tree-nail driven in, on which hung a tackle block.

He was induced from the appearance to suppose that it might be the place referred to by the sailor. He then acquainted two men, Smith and Vaughn, of the circumstance, and they commenced digging.

After going down ten feet they found a layer of oak timber, at twenty the same, and thirty the same. By this time the work became too heavy for them to carry on alone, and they tried to get the inhabitants to join them; but they refused from a kind of superstitious dread.

(MY NOTE: This is the first recorded mention of any kind of superstition associated with Oak Island. Whatever caused this had to have happened before the original Money Pit excavation began.)

About seven years afterwards, Simeon Lynds of Onslow went down to Chester, and happening to stop with Mr. Vaughn, he was informed of what had taken place. He then agreed to get up a company, which he did, of about 25 or 30 men, and they commenced where the first left off, and sunk the pit 93 feet, finding a mark every ten feet. Some of them were charcoal, some putty, and one at 80 feet was a stone cut square, two feet long and about a foot thick, with several characters on it.

All the way down they were confined to a diameter of 16 feet, by the softness of the ground within that limit. The pick marks could be distinctly seen all around the sides of the pit. After they got down 93 feet, they forced a crowbar down and struck wood at five which appeared to be a platform from its being level, making in all to the supposed platform 98 feet.

They then quit the work until morning, when on commencing again they found the pit filled with water, as high as the tide level. They then tried bailing and afterwards tried pumping which was all to no purpose. After which they sank a new pit in order to tunnel under the treasure which was unsuccessful.

Matters stood so until 1849, when a few persons in Truro, hearing Lynds tell the story, got up a company.

They got down to 86 feet, when the water drove them out. They then bored.

This part of the work I can speak of with more certainty than any previous, as I took part in it personally, and worked on the auger.

(MY NOTE: McCully is sometimes given as the "Manager of Operations" for the Truro Company).

We bored five holes, in the first of which we lost the only valve sludger we had. It was a long pod with a valve at the bottom to prevent the contents from dropping out. This we always used after the chisel. It was lost by being a little too rash, and thereby twisting it off at the shank.

Having lost it we had only one left, which had, instead of a valve, a ball inside with a pin across the bottom to keep the ball from dropping out. That one would not admit of coin passing into it.

It would seem strange that we should not have got another valve sludger, but people who are penny wise and pound foolish sometimes do strange things. I wanted the persons in charge to send for two or three, but could not prevail on them to do so.

The second hole we bored struck the platform which the old diggers told us about -- precisely at the depth they told us they had struck it with the crowbar, 98 feet.

It proved to be spruce, six inches thick. After the auger went through it, it dropped one foot and struck wood again, which was oak, four inches thick, then twenty inches of metal in small pieces which we knew from the sound and from the fact that the auger would go through by simply turning it – then eight inches oak, then 20 inches metal, then four inches oak, six inches spruce, and then seven feet worked clay, then hard clay which had never been disturbed, another of the five holes struck the platform at the same depth, 98 feet; after going through the auger dropped a little more than it did in the first hole, and struck a cask which was evident from our bringing up a piece of an oak stave, and some pieces of birch hoops.

We also brought three small links which had apparently been forced from an epulette (more typically spelled "epaulette"). *They were gold.*

After that another gang bored, but the results were known only to the person who conducted the boring, which he managed to keep to himself. But a short time after, he made such disclosures to Mr. Charles D. Archibald, who was then concerned in the Londonderry Iron Mines, that he, Mr. A, went to the Government and got a license to dig. But from our having applied for a license before, they could only get permission to dig on unoccupied ground, which kept them from doing anything while our lease held good.

One of the parties dying in the meantime, and Mr. A. being in Europe, they did not avail themselves of the license. Our company worked at it for four years, during which time they found a drain, or tunnel, leading from the sea to the pit. By digging a pit about 20 feet from the old pit and 94 feet deep, also near the shores at the same level, which would make it appear that the water came into the old pit about the top of the upper platform.

Work was evidently done by hands in both pits, and also at the beach, where we found flag stones made in the form of drains and covered with a type of grass, not the growth of this country, and the outer rind of the cocoanut. When the drain was struck in the pits, in both cases, the water burst in with such force as to drive us out.

We drove piles into the one at the shore to stop the course of the water which slackened the flow of water in the old money pit but did not stop it altogether, thereby inducing us to believe that there might be another drain.

We afterwards dug two other pits near the old money pit, and found that there was no difficulty from the water at 109 and 112 feet until we attempted to work into the old pit by tunnelling, when it would invariably rise to a level with the tide. That company also gave up, and last summer we formed another, and commenced digging a new pit 120 feet deep about 25 feet from the old money pit. Our object was to intercept the water but to no purpose; we then tunnelled from one of the old pits on the west side, in order to enter the money pit, between the upper and lower platform, but from a misunderstanding about the starting point, the tunnel entered the old money pit a little below the lower platform, where we found the soft clay spoken of in the boring.

The tunnel was unwisely driven through the old pit until it nearly reached the east pipe, when the water started, apparently, coming above as on the east side.

We then bailed from the west pit, with six horses, for three days, and the horses becoming tired for want of oats, of which we ran short, we knocked off, and went home, and started again with 33 horses and over 60 men.

We then rigged gins and a bailing apparatus on the new pit, the money pit, and the west pit, and commenced bailing on Wednesday morning, continuing constantly night and day, until Friday morning, when the tunnel leading from the west pit to the money pit, which was 17 feet long, 4 feet high, and three feet wide, becoming choked with clay, we sent two men down to clear it out. After they had gone about half way through they heard a tremendous crash in the money pit, and barely escaped being caught by a rush of mud which followed them into the west pit, and filled it up seven feet in less than three minutes.

In the mean time a stick of oak timber of considerable girth and 3 1-2 feet in length, was ejected with the mud, all of which was soon cut up and made into walking canes, one of which I have the pleasure of sending you.

The bailing continued until three o'clock, p.m., of Saturday, when, on clearing the tunnel again, another crash was heard in the money pit, which we supposed to be the upper platform falling, and immediately the bottom of the money pit fell to about 102 feet, measuring from the level of the ground at the top.

It had been cleared out previously down 88 feet. Immediately after, the cribbing of the money pit, commencing at the bottom, fell in, plank after plank, until there was only about thirty feet of the upper cribbing left. On Monday the top fell in, leaving the old money pit a complete mass of ruins. We then got a cast iron pump and steam engine from Chebucto Foundry in Halifax; but the boilers being defective we were obliged to give up, after spending considerable time etc., until the Spring of this year – not, however, until we proved that the water could be pumped out in two hours.

We now talk of letting a job of the whole work to Sutherland & Co., railway contractors, who have agreed to finish the work to our satisfaction, according to specification, for $4000, and which will take all the risk or forfeit payment, for which purpose we are now endeavouring to raise the required amount of stock. The foregoing statement can be certified on oath of respectable persons. Now, I leave the matter to a discerning public, to say, whether we are the fools some people take us to be, in endeavouring to set the question for ever at rest. But I suppose the public will judge of it by the success we meet with. Should we be successful in getting a large amount of treasure we will be considered a very sensible lot of fellows; and if we should fail in finishing the work we will be set down as a set of phantom-following fools, fit for nothing but to be held up to public ridicule.

But facts are stubborn things. We have proved that the old "money pit," so called, was dug, and that the water must have been let into it after it was filled up.

The filling of it, leaving the ten feet marks, shows that the water did not flow into it until after it was filled; also, that the tunnel must have been made before it was filled, and that probably the last thing they did was to tear away a dam and let on the water. By the way the remains of an old dam was seen outside of the place where we found the drain and tunnel on the shore.

Yours, Etc, J.B. McCully

I'm not sure I can add much to McCully's detailed description of the earliest digs, unmatched by any other. Oak Island fans are so lucky to have these records.

According to McCully, it appears, at least at face value, that digging was done by hand. However, it also appears that in 1849 the first boring or drilling was done.

McCully mentions a sludge valve and so I took a look into this. From a book on mining written in 1888, just 26 years after McCully's letter, I found two illustrations similar to what would have been used on Oak Island. One is of a valve sludger (far left) which McCully said had broken on them; the other is a ball valve sludger which McCully said did not allow coins to enter past the ball valve in order to be inspected on the surface.

The following is from the 1888 book: "The sludger is worked by jerking it up and down in the bore-hole. During the descent of the tool, the valve is raised by the water in the hole. The weight of the sludger causes it to sink into the debris which is thus forced above the valve. As the sludger ascends, the material which has entered acts with the water to close the valve. By this means the escape of the sludge is prevented, though a large portion of the water passes out through the accidental interstices occasioned by small pieces of stone upon the valve seating."

The article notes: "The debris brought up from the bottom of the bore-hole by the sludger must be treated with careful attention, for it must be borne in mind that in prospecting for minerals it is to obtain this debris that the boring is undertaken."

The same would hold true for any treasure or coins that might be brought up from the Money Pit.

The "gold chains" from the epaulette that McCully said was recovered may have looked like those on the image shown here.

A gold craftsman of the day told McCully that he felt the chains were likely made of an alloy of gold and copper.

While it seems, up to this point, that the digging was done by hand, horse-powered pumps were kept running quite often to keep the inflow of water low enough to work. When digging was not an option, the searchers turned to boring holes with mine drilling equipment.

Pointed augers would cut through the dirt and debris. If sludge was encountered, the sludge valves were attached to the drill instead, to painstakingly clear the sludge and search it for any treasures. This work must have taken some real patience.

Since McCully's letter was written in 1862, 1861 would be the year the bottom literally fell out of the Money Pit. He describes three different collapses. Most of what he is talking about, though, is the cribbing placed in the Money Pit by searchers to keep the sides from collapsing.

So it was not truly the original Money Pit collapsing, except perhaps in the collapse where the Money Pit bottom fell from the 88 feet level, which had already been excavated, down to 102 foot – a drop of 14 feet, indicating some type of cavity below the original floor of the pit. The *Liverpool Transcript* newspaper of August 29, 1861 states that "many (people) were badly injured."

Water and collapsing dirt have plagued the Money Pit search ever since. It seems no matter how sophisticated the equipment gets, the same two problems exist. Robert Dunfield's 1960s search was stopped short by muddy conditions as was one or more of the big canister digs by the current search team. You may remember the dramatic moment when one of the Michigan Group's big boring machines nearly collapsed into the Money Pit area.

This is why the current treasure seekers have turned to alternative ways to see what is below the surface with the occasional test bore holes and even some gigantic canister bore holes.

Just about every method of exploring the island through sounding devices, LIDAR, ground penetrating radar, ROVs, or even real life divers has been used. Enough tantalizing items have been brought to the surface to prove that something was buried at fairly great depth in the Money Pit area.

Mapping of this area has been, and is being done, to determine where all the searcher shafts and, hopefully, the original shafts are.

One issue is that the drill borings don't always travel straight down, giving false depth readings and intersecting with other previous bore holes. Still, the work goes on and discoveries continue to be made, many of which support my 1632 theory.

All carbon dating adds in a plus or minus range of possible dates. One reason for this variance is simply because it can't always be determined when the wood was used by a human as opposed to when the tree died.

The very first known carbon dated wood from Oak Island has been shown to accommodate my 1632 date, and the pattern has repeated itself many times.

Carbon dating technology was born in 1946. By 1969, samples of hand worked wood found "at depth" (below ground, beyond where wood would normally be expected to be discovered) were carbon dated to 1575, plus or minus 85 years. This fits my 1632 date.

In 1981, two sets of samples were sent for carbon dating and returned dates of 1700, plus or minus 80 years, and 1670, plus or minus 70 years. Both of these windows fit my 1632 date. This was just the beginning!

During the more modern searches, a piece of axe-cut wood found in 2019, at depth in the vicinity of the Money Pit, dated to as old as 1626. In 2020, a T-square uncovered in the swamp dated to as old as 1632 – exactly my target date. In 2021, a ship part from the swamp dated to 1520-1674. Also, two chunks of wood found at depth in two separate test drill holes had identical carbon dates of between 1488 and 1650, equally allowing for my target year. In addition, a root was found under the "stone road" in the Oak Island swamp that had a carbon dating of 1474 to 1638, also allowing for my 1632 date.

These are just a few of the biological items that have carbon dated to a window which supports my theory. Other items not able to be carbon dated also support my target year. They include shoes found near a sunken wharf that were dated before 1700 based on peg construction techniques, along with a pair of scissors dated by the Smithsonian to the 1600s. In addition, two items were dated by blacksmith Carmen Legge – a Scottish ox shoe dating to as early as 1610, and a woodworking adze tool dating to as early as 1620. Several metal spikes and square nails, plus random pieces of metal were also estimated to date into the 1600s based on their metal alloy content and design. Carmen stated, based on his experience, that he sees a definite time period on Oak Island of metal artifacts dating from about 1610 through 1650.

One of the few pieces of actual treasure found on Oak Island was a garnet pin which, based on its rudimentary cut, was dated to be around 400-500 years old. More recently, a piece of a flintlock rifle was found. The first flintlock was not invented until 1630, meaning this piece could not have been left on Oak Island before that date.

These are only a few examples of the many artifacts that have been found that could fit my 1632 theory.

In further support of the 1632 date, Gilbert Hedden, who owned Oak Island in the 1930s, estimated the date of the Money Pit creation to be as early as 1635 (in a letter written to President Franklin Roosevelt) and again "around 1630" (in a letter to an Oak Island fan written in 1967). Plus, the oldest known deed or land charter for the area surrounding Oak Island dates to 1630, and there is plenty of evidence of Scottish activity in Nova Scotia from 1623 through 1632.

If my theory and my newest translation of the 90' Stone are correct, they fit in exactly with the history of Nova Scotia, Scotland, England and France, plus the history of the beginnings of Freemasonry, and the histories of the people involved in my Oak Island theory.

I don't believe there is any other Oak Island theory or any other 90' Stone translation that is supported by this much evidence. Because my theories and research are unique it takes awhile for the typical Oak Island enthusiast to get their minds off Knights Templar or pirate answers to the mystery. But, given a chance, I believe my books reveal a story much closer to the truth, where Oak Island is involved.

Chapter Four

STONES AND CODES

Did the 90' Stone really exist? Jotham McCully was first to mention it in print, but not the only one.

McCully was intricately tied to the Money Pit dig as a Manager of Operations at some point for at least one of two Truro groups (1848-1862), and Corporate Secretary for the Oak Island Association (1863-1866). As we have seen, the first known mention of the 90' Stone was in the letter from June 2, 1862, written by McCully.

The earliest mention of the Money Pit was made in an October 1856 issue of the *Liverpool Transcript* newspaper. More articles on the "Oak Island Follies" appeared as early as August 1857, explaining the first line of McCully's letter stating: "Having been ridiculed by the press..."

There are at least three reasons why the 90' Stone can be thought of as real but just didn't get reported on until several years later:

1) There were no Nova Scotia newspapers at the time of the 90' Stone discovery and absolutely no photography for many years to come. The *Nova Scotia Packet* news sheet ceased publication in 1796. The *Acadian Recorder* newspaper began publication in 1813. There were no known Nova Scotia newspapers between these dates, when the 90' Stone was found in 1804.

The *Liverpool Transcript*, in which McCully's letter appeared, began publication in 1854. The Money Pit was mentioned in an 1856 edition, and the 90' Stone in 1862.

Also, an article from January 2, 1864, in *The Colonist* newspaper, written by one of the members of the Oak Island Association, states: "Further down was a flagstone about two feet long and one wide, with a number of rudely cut letters and figures upon it. They were in hopes this inscription would throw some valuable light on their search, but unfortunately they could not decipher it, as it was either too badly cut or did not appear to be in their own vernacular. **This remarkable stone was pretty far down in the pit, laying in the centre with the engraved side down.** As it was preserved in the family of Mr. Smith, **it may be seen by the curious at the present day.**" Note the words "present day." The stone was later taken from John Smith's home to Halifax in 1865.

2) The stone was reportedly viewed by many people in a bookbinder's window, and there is an unverified drawing and also a photograph of the stone found online. In 1935, Oak Island searcher Fred Blair was told by Harry Marshall that he actually saw the stone in 1919.

3) There was no easy way to share the discovery with the world. It didn't help that there was no real Nova Scotia Historical Society between 1804 and 1878. The fact that the stone is now missing is not surprising at all. Throughout history plenty of people have snatched up unique items. In fact, recently a collector in New York was forced to give up 180 very rare artifacts that he had acquired from around the world, worth $70 million.

Based on what I've discovered about the 90' Stone, I wouldn't be at all surprised if a Freemason has it.

There are three versions of the 90' Stone's code:

1) The first is the Rev. Austen Kempton 90' Stone cipher. He received this code in 1909 and showed it to Oak Island legend Frederick Blair and to New England author Edward Snow in 1949. Kempton graduated from Acadia University and was a respected minister with nothing to gain from lying about the stone or the code.

2) Edward Snow, a famous author of many books, also with nothing to gain by lying about the stone, published his rendition of the cipher with the second character missing and most of the slanting of the symbols from the Kempton cipher straightened up, except the downward arrow in line one. The second character on the stone was also eliminated in the "Forty feet below..." translation.

3) The above more-modern rendition of the stone stays faithful to the Kempton and Snow ciphers except for the final character, and another one like it in the sixth line. Both are shown as a rectangular box instead of what appears to be similar to the Roman numeral for two (2) shown on the Kempton and Snow versions. This character becomes an important part of my translation.

It has never made sense to me that the 90' Stone contained instructions on how to retrieve the Money Pit treasure since it was found so deep underground. If you wanted your followers to find a treasure, the instructions would need to be placed near the top of the Money Pit.

My translation differs from all others in three ways. No one else, to my knowledge, has ever proposed any of these methods for translating the 90' Stone:

1) Instead of a simple letter substitution, my translation substitutes complete words for each symbol;

2) My translation presents the message as something other than instructions on how to dig up the treasure;

3) My translation uses a well-known, famous code that matches virtually every symbol on the 90' Stone.

Stones have often been considered to have special and sometimes magical properties. In addition to the curse stones I've already mentioned, other examples include:

- The Irish Blarney Stone
- The Scottish Stone of Destiny
- The Philosopher's Stone
- Crystals and Amulets
- King Arthur's sword stone
- Stonehenge (and many other megalithic stones)

Some significant stones from my theory include the Masonic cornerstone, plus a stone found in the treasure stolen by Al Strachan, and two stones mentioned in the very last letter ever written by the famous Mary, Queen of Scots, known in the research world as MQS. I'll be mentioning Mary, Queen of Scots, a lot in this chapter.

A cornerstone was, and still is, sometimes considered a powerful ceremonial step in building a substantial structure, especially by Freemasons. Its orientation had to be placed just right, it had to be level and square, and often it would contain items hidden inside. A number of curious stones have been found on Oak Island that might be connected to Freemasonry.

Below is a line from the list of treasure stolen by Al Strachan in 1622 (the partner of William Alexander, founder of Nova Scotia or New Scotland) in which appears the mention of a healing stone with considerable worth attached to it: "Ane jasp stone for steming of bluid (a supposed healing stone) estimated at 500 French crowns..." (about $18,000 in U.S. dollars today).

This shows that even possibly the richest man in all of Scotland in 1622 thought that a stone could have power of its own and be worth a lot of money. This belief extended even to royalty.

Shown here is the very last letter of MQS (Mary, Queen of Scots) written shortly before her execution giving "two precious stones, talismans against illness" to her brother-in-law, King Henry III of France. I'll have many other words from MQS to show and explain my 90' Stone translation.

What if the 90' Stone was actually a curse or prayer stone believed to have had some special power, and was left behind with the Oak Island treasure to protect it, not to describe how to find it?

Thousands of so-called curse tablets have been found buried around the world, especially in Israel, Egypt, Greece, Rome and the British Isles. Some are carved or chiseled into stone as with the 90' Stone. Most are in the nature of a curse, but some also call on "holy beings," more like a prayer.

I have discovered a cipher codex created by Mary, Queen of Scots, which contains a complete word for virtually every symbol from the 90' Stone! In fact, I own the most complete digitized collection in the world of MQS coded letters and cipher codex sheets which were digitized exclusively for me by the National Archives of the United Kingdom. In all, there are 104 sheets that contain her codes. The obvious question here is what would Mary, Queen of Scots, have to do with the 90' Stone found on Oak Island.

Mary created a very complex, highly-regarded cipher codex featured on several code-breaking websites even today. She was also the progenitor of four successive kings of Great Britain, all involved with Nova Scotia.

Her son, James I of England and Ireland (James VI of Scotland), chartered Nova Scotia to William Alexander in 1621. Her grandson, Charles I of Great Britain, knighted all the Knights Baronet of Nova Scotia from 1625 until his execution in 1649. In addition, Mary's great grandson, Charles II, knighted Thomas Temple, the very last Knight Baronet of Nova Scotia to be given land (land which included Oak Island). Another great grandson, James II, knighted William Phips, who has often been associated with Oak Island and now, through my research, with nearby New Ross. I wrote extensively about Phips in my *Oak Island Knights* book, back in 2019.

If a stone was to be coded and left behind in the Money Pit by representatives of one of these four kings, why not use a cipher that was already "in the family" – one that used unique methods to hide a secret message?

Mary, Queen of Scots, was an extremely powerful person, at least for a good share of her short life. The only child of her father, James V of Scotland, she was bound to be Queen of Scotland when he died. That much happened. However, in the meantime, she was married to Francis, the Dauphin (Prince) of France, who died very young, shortly after ascending to the throne of France.

The brother of Francis followed him as King of France even though Mary should have remained as Queen of France as well as Queen of Scotland. Several written notations refer to her as Mary, Queen of Scotland, France and England. The reason she was thought of as a possible Queen of England (and Ireland) was that her cousin Queen Elizabeth had no children to follow her, and Mary, Queen of Scotland and France, would be next in line as Queen of England as well, which would be a first for these countries to be united under one ruler.

This possible succession route made MQS someone to contend with. The problem for Mary was that she was Catholic and, when she returned to Scotland, she began being challenged by Presbyterian forces. She stood strong for a long time and went through a variety of challenges too complex for this book to tell. She eventually took refuge with her cousin, Queen Elizabeth, in hopes that the queen would show mercy on her own kin.

Many historians feel that Elizabeth, jealous of Mary and of the son she had left behind in Scotland, had her imprisoned for several years and eventually beheaded. The stated reason for the beheading lay in the secret code Mary was using to communicate with her supporters.

That code has become known as the "MQS code" and, until recently, only a couple of pages were available for the public to see. I spent several months and wrote many emails trying to track down any other MQS codex sheets that might exist. I was looking in the wrong place.

After exhausting every contact I had in the historical societies of Scotland, it was suggested that I approach the National Archives of the United Kingdom. Turns out they had all of Mary's papers that were confiscated when she was arrested. There were over four hundred sheets.

I asked if they could possibly sort out only those sheets that had any hint of a code on them, which they did. In the end, there were an additional 102 coded papers. For a fee they scanned these into a digital form for me to download, making my collection the first, and perhaps still the exclusive and most complete digital collection of Mary's handiwork at code usage.

Understanding these codes is an ongoing process, but it soon became obvious that nearly every symbol on the 90' Stone from the Oak Island Money Pit was also found on the MQS codex sheets. You can imagine my excitement when I shared this with the Oak Island team.

I spent weeks meticulously translating the stone code, all the while wondering at what I was finding and why I was finding it. On the latter question, I believe this code was used simply because it was Mary's descendants who were involved with Nova Scotia during the 1600s. It would make sense that they and their associates would be familiar enough with the code to use it since her life and story were still fresh in the minds of Great Britain.

Proof of this is that in 1624, the same year William Alexander wrote his book on Nova Scotia, another book was published entitled *The Historie of the Life and Death of Mary Stuart Queene of Scotland.* It was dedicated to Mary's son, King James VI of Scotland, and now King James I of England and Ireland as well. Books during this period were rare and very expensive to produce. They were seldom if ever profitable, so dedicating them to a person of means allowed that person to foot most of the bill. This means that King James likely paid for this history of his own mother's life and death.

There was so much hidden and secretive in those days that often the true author would even use an alias. In the case of this book, he used the name "Wil. Stranguage," as in "Strange-language."

Certainly the MQS code is a strange language. He reprinted the book under his real name a few years later – William Udall. He begins the book:

Mary, Queen of Scots

O, the Sepulchers of our Ancestors, how much more doe they teach than all the studie, bookes and precepts of the learned! And herein due praise must needs be ascribed vnto Historie, (and) *the life of memorie...*

Mary, Queen of Scots' life and death were still on many people's minds at the time of the Knights Baronet attempt to settle Nova Scotia. So there is every reason to believe that whoever placed the 90' Stone in the Money Pit could have used a well-known and famous code, especially if told to do so by one of her descendants, four of them being successive kings of Great Britain.

Present at the trial of Mary, Queen of Scots, were two men significant to my story. The first was Nicholas Bacon, father of Sir Francis Bacon, a man who has been connected with Oak Island in many ways, and who was certainly a friend of William Alexander.

Francis Bacon died at the home of Thomas Howard, Earl of Arundel. Thomas was the grandson of our second significant man, Thomas Howard, the Duke of Norfolk, who served as the Principal of the Commission at York, in 1568, to hear evidence against Mary, Queen of Scots.

Just four years later the elder Duke Thomas Howard was put to death when it was alleged that he had plotted against Queen Elizabeth and had secretly tried to win the hand of Mary, Queen of Scots, in marriage.

The Howard name is new to Oak Island legend, but you will soon see how it ties in as deeply as any name possibly could.

Despite the Duke of Norfolk's participation at the trial, he was secretly a staunch supporter of Mary, Queen of Scots, and wanted to marry her. He was the *paternal* grandfather and namesake of the younger Thomas Howard, Earl of Arundel, and was the wealthiest landowner in the entire country of Great Britain.

The father of Thomas Howard, Earl of Arundel, was named Philip, and he also died accused of treason. He was actually made a saint – St. Philip Howard.

Thomas's great-grandfather, Henry, Earl of Surrey, (also executed for treason) is credited with introducing the rhyming scheme which now characterizes the typical Shakespearean sonnet. Henry Howard of Surrey was married to Frances de Vere whose own brother, Edward, is suspected of writing some of Shakespeare's plays.

Thomas Howard, Earl of Arundel, was a patron of William Shakespeare and presented some of his plays to the king, and at other venues. Howard is thought to have met face-to-face with Shakespeare on many occasions.

Both William Alexander and Francis Bacon have also been connected to Shakespeare's plays as possible secret authors. Howard, Bacon and Alexander all lived within a short walk of Shakespeare's Globe Theatre.

King James I, and later King Charles I, were regular visitors at Thomas Howard's home, and King James was actually the godfather of Howard's eldest son, Henry.

This father and son team, Thomas and Henry Howard, is about to make it into Oak Island history with the revealing of my MQS translation of the 90' Stone.

Thomas Howard, Earl of Arundel, lived and died near Charing Cross, London, as did William Alexander, founder of Nova Scotia. Sir Francis Bacon was born near Charing Cross and died there as well, in Howard's home. The only other place in all of the world and in all of history ever to be called Charing Cross is New Ross, Nova Scotia. (See my book *Oak Island And New Ross*).

Thomas Howard, Sir Francis Bacon, and Sir William Alexander were all involved in the Plymouth Colony. Howard, in fact, signed the petition to reform the Plymouth Company just two signatures below that of Sir Francis Bacon. He then prosecuted Bacon on possibly phony bribery charges, although the two men remained friends afterwards. Howard also served on a committee which took over Bacon's duties as Lord Chancellor. In addition, he was named Earl Marshal of England in this year – the top law enforcement officer.

Thomas Howard, Earl of Arundel's name also appears on Sir William Alexander's 1624 map of Nova Scotia. Recently, I found out that Thomas Howard and William Alexander were both leaders of a Council on Fishing which began in July 1632, one month after Alexander's people returned from Nova Scotia, after being ousted by the French. I will have much more on this short-lived, possibly secret spy organization, coming up.

In 1626, Sir Francis Bacon died at the home of Thomas Howard, Earl of Arundel. This is an incredible link of Thomas Howard to one of the more prominent Money Pit theories – that Bacon's or Shakespeare's papers were buried there. Between his death at Howard's home and the fact that Howard took over part of his position as Lord Chancellor after Bacon's trial, Howard had the opportunity to collect some, if not many, of Bacon's papers as well. It is also possible that Howard had some of Mary, Queen of Scots' codex sheets in his collection since his grandfather prosecuted and yet supported her, and also used this same MQS code for his own purposes.

In the same 1624 book about Mary, Queen of Scots, where I found that Nicholas Bacon and Duke Thomas Howard were both on the team to prosecute Mary, I also found the following about Duke Thomas Howard's own trial for secretly supporting Mary:

Gerard, the Queen's attorney (Queen Elizabeth) *said: "It is most apparent that he did purposely aim to marry the Queen of Scotland to work the Queen's* (Elizabeth again) *destruction. It is also apparent that he did advisedly consult of invading the realm by the letters to the pope, the King of Spain and the Duke of Alba. All his dealings with Ridolph are now well known by the secret ciphers and characterical notes hidden under the tiles of Howard House."*

Thomas Howard, Duke of Norfolk, grandfather to Thomas Howard, Earl of Arundel, used the MQS code for his own purposes and was caught with it in his house, buried under his floor tile. There is another example from Mary's biography that reads:

And shortly after, the Duke (Thomas Howard, Duke of Norfolk) *requested him, by his cipher letters to give his consent to the marriage* (with MQS).

This proves that the elder Howard was using Mary's code for his own secret letters. The MQS code could be no more closely connected to the Howard family if we tried. By the way, the definition of the word "characterical," from an online dictionary states: "Late 16th century; earliest use found in Timothy Bright... Partly from character + -ical."

In the shorthand system devised by Timothy Bright, certain words can be written as single characters or symbols. This is exactly what I believe the 90' Stone code to be – individual symbols meant to replace complete words. And nearly all of the 90' Stone symbols also appear on the codex created by Mary, Queen of Scots, and used by Thomas Howard, Duke of Norfolk, her secret supporter.

According to the 1624 history of Mary, Queen of Scots, in her closet, upon her arrest, were found "about 60 kinds of ciphers." The cipher sheets that I purchased from the National Archives of the United Kingdom consist of 104 sheets, but in sorting through them, many contain so few ciphers as to be useless. In the end, I would guess that "about 60 kinds of ciphers" would describe my main collection of useful cipher sheets, meaning I must now own them all.

These ciphers are not easy to read and some are in French, but the symbols I've discovered so far, that were used on the 90' Stone, are fairly simple to translate. This would indicate that whoever used the MQS code was not an expert in it, but simply used the easiest ciphers to mark the 90' Stone, perhaps even in honor of Mary.

In a strange twist of possible support for my theory, David Neisen, a retired intelligence analyst, has taken a deep dive into the story behind the Oak Island "oak" trees. He was somewhat stunned to find an almost identical row of trees on an island in Scotland. He is currently writing a book about his discoveries but has given me permission to report on part of his research.

David enlisted assistance from a Scottish botanist, Stephen Bungard, who studied these Scottish trees found in MacDonald / McGinnis territory. While I don't want to steal his thunder by telling the complete tale, I will reveal one photo which shows a pair of trees copied from the Scottish grove and pasted into an empty spot on an old photo of the Oak Island trees. I've included an arrow pointing to the newly inserted trees because, without it, I don't believe anyone would be able to tell the difference!

Neisen also provided a copy of an email conversation he had with Mr. Bungard, who believes the trees to be a certain species of European Sycamore.

Bungard made the statement concerning this species that: "Sycamore trees were widely associated with the French connections of Mary, Queen of Scots. A tree planted by Mary, at Scone Palace, stood till 1941, when it fell in a storm." Note, the Oak Island trees were reported to be on their last legs by 1934, and gone by 1945.

Neisen's own analysis, at least at this point, is that, based on the typical age to which these trees are known to live, "The Oak Island trees could have been planted anytime before 1752, and as early as 1622." David made this assessment well before learning of my *Oak Island 1632* book, or my early 17th century Oak Island theory.

Chapter Five
MY TRANSLATION

There are three things that set the MQS code apart from a simple letter substitution codex.

One feature that made Mary, Queen of Scots's cipher code particularly difficult to crack and somewhat unique is that she used the "characterical" system of replacing a complete word with a symbol. All the symbols found on the 90' Stone, except one for "Scottish Master," match symbols found in her code, and spell out some interesting sentences using complete word substitutions.

Second, she used symbols that she referred to as "nulles" or as we would write it today, "nulls." These were selected symbols with no meaning whatsoever, which were inserted into a line of code to confuse the code breaker. These are still used in sophisticated codes even today.

Another trick she used was the addition of symbols for "puncturing" the code, which is a concept I admit to not completely understanding, although it is also a technique still used in modern code writing.

Despite all of these tricks, it was still not too difficult for me to translate a fair amount of the 90' Stone code, though I also admit to not completely understanding its message yet. Still, there's enough to wet our whistles.

Although MQS had a dozen or so "null" ciphers listed on her various codex sheets, the first one listed on her most commonly referred to sheet (as well as on three additional sheets) is shown below. Keep in mind, this was written by her hand about 450 years ago:

The most commonly used symbol from the 90' Stone code is shown next:

The similarity between these two symbols is worth noting, especially considering they were written/carved by two different people perhaps a hundred or more years apart, then transcribed by a third and fourth person a few hundred years later. It would seem likely that the most commonly used symbol in a line of code would also be a null in order to fool the code breaker early on, and often.

Another 90' Stone code breaker, Daniel Ronnstam, (who has also presented his code translation in the War Room) eliminated this symbol as well, referring to it as an "arithmetic symbol" marking the end of the phrases on the stone. Whether we eliminate it or not from the final translation, it would not change the phrases where it is found that dramatically, since we are translating each symbol as a word, rather than a single letter. If, as Ronnstam proposed, they were just meant to be a sort of punctuation, they would still fit my translation well.

Below, once again, is Edward Snow's rendition of the 90' Stone after consulting with Rev. Kempton and seeing first hand the code that Kempton was given in 1909.

Once the suspected null symbol is removed, the code shown below contains the final symbols needed to translate the 90' Stone cipher, and would consist of eight lines, perhaps completing three or four sentences.

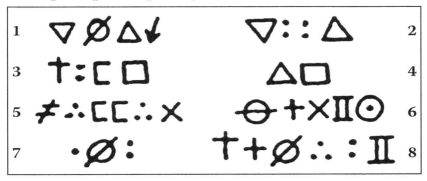

Including the null, EVERY SINGLE SYMBOL on the 90' Stone code is also represented on the MQS codex, except one. That one remaining symbol (found three times on the stone) is the three dot triangle, the Masonic symbol for "Scottish Master of Masons," still in use today. It has been right in front of everyone's eyes for over two centuries and only revealed now in my book.

As you view the translation of the first line of the 90'
Stone, keep in mind the invoking of "holy beings" or
God found in the first line of many curse or prayer
tablets over the last two millennia.

▽ = O   ϕ = *Intelligence*   ▲ = *send*   ↓ = *Angels*

Working from right to left using the actual handwriting
of Mary, Queen of Scots, the word "Angels" is obvious,
as is the word "send."

The word "Intelligence" is one of the few capitalized
words on Mary's actual codex besides the word Angels
(plus the names of a few specific people). Even though
she died for her religion, she had no code for the names
God or Jesus. However, she did have a separate code for
"intelligence" with a lower case beginning. This leads
me to believe that this second symbol in line one is
meant to represent "God," as in Supreme Intelligence.

The word "O" is a supplication, as in O, *Canada* or in
"O, say can you see?" This differs from "Oh," which is
an exclamation, as in "Oh! I forgot my keys." And who
is the typical object of a supplication if not God?

The resulting translation of line one from the 90'
Stone, using the MQS codex, is in perfect keeping with
the first line of other curse/prayer stones found
throughout the world that were buried with belongings
or land markers, and requested Heavenly help:

O, GOD SEND ANGELS

"O, God send angels" is also in keeping with many phrases from the Bible and other religious texts where the concept of God sending angels to help mankind is very common and a main form of interaction and intercession between God and the human race.

You may remember, I believe the Oak Island mystery began with a Scotsman named William Alexander who rose to the highest ranks of government in England and played an important role in the formation of Freemasonry. He was given Nova Scotia in 1621 by King James I, son of Mary, Queen of Scots. He struggled for the next four years to gather the money and settlers necessary to take advantage of his large unspoiled realm.

In 1625, Alexander created the Knights Baronet of Nova Scotia. Each knight would pay a fee for this honor and provide six men with skills to settle this new land.

But before all that could happen, both Alexander and King James came under severe financial difficulties. This is recorded in many places. In 1622, the king actually demanded loans of his richer subjects giving them jewels as collateral. For his part, Alexander complained many times about not being able to raise funds.

Also, in 1622, Alexander (Al) Strachan robbed perhaps the richest man in Scotland of his treasure and his wife. He remained under indictment for a few years until King James pardoned him. Sir William Alexander then accepted him as a partner, and Strachan became one of the very first Knights Baronet of Nova Scotia.

So, to find the following words in line five of the 90' Stone code would not be out of line with my theory.

We have five specific words of interest here. The first two are the words "Great (and) Treasure," the third is the Masonic code for "Scottish Master of Masons," fourth is "Scotland," and the fifth word is "Edinburgh."

We once again have these symbols, shown below, with the words they represent. All but the three dot triangle were written by Mary, Queen of Scots. It is not surprising that Mary spelled "great" and "treasure" differently than we do today. Even now, many words are spelled differently in Great Britain and Canada than in the U.S., and time has led to refined spelling in all English speaking nations.

$\mp$ = *gret Tresawrare*

Edinburgh = ▫

⊏ = *Scotland*

The three dot triangle is a Masonic symbol originally representing the "Scottish Master of Masons" and is found three times on the 90′ Stone. We now have some significantly translated words that easily fit my theory:

GREAT TREASURE,

SCOTTISH MASTER,

EDINBURGH, SCOTLAND

While I have more work to do to make sense of the entire 90' Stone code, the next two lines, numbered six and eight, mirror each other to a large degree and open up an entirely new chapter in the saga of Oak Island.

I've written a lot about Thomas Howard, Earl of Arundel, earlier in this book, and now you are about to find out why. On her codex, Mary had symbols listed as representing several people. Two of these people were Thomas Howard, Earl of Arundel, and his son Lord Henry Howard. Here are their symbols in Mary's very own handwriting:

✛ = *the Earle of Arrondel*

Ⅱ = *the Lo: H: Haward*

She also had symbols for "so," "not" and "will":

⊖ = *so*   ✕ = not   ☉ = wiℓℓ

Therefore we have a complete and simple translation of line six from the 90" Stone.

SO, THE EARL OF ARUNDEL, NOT HENRY HOWARD, WILL.

What exactly is meant by this I cannot yet say, but it is certain that the names of these two men are mentioned using the MQS code, and I have otherwise connected Thomas Howard with the Plymouth Colony and Nova Scotia, and with William Alexander, Sir Francis Bacon, Shakespeare, Charing Cross, Kings James I and Charles I of Great Britain and, most importantly, Freemasonry.

Using some of the same 90' Stone symbols and adding in three additional symbols, we have a repeat of the names of both father and son, Thomas and Henry Howard, on line eight. The additional symbols are:

† = *support*   **:** = *and*

•
∴ =   Though not found on Mary, Queen of Scots' codex, this
• •   symbol originally meant Scottish Master of Masons,
         and is still used in Freemasonry to mean Master Mason.

Using the symbols taken directly from the 90' Stone as translated by the symbols taken directly from the MQS code, we also have an easy translation of the final line:

$$† + \emptyset \therefore : \amalg$$

Support the Earl of Arundel, God, the Scottish Master of Masons, and (His Son) Henry Howard.

The X is represented in most cases within the MQS codex sheets as the word "not." The **:** (or colon) is represented as the word "and." It is also used to separate closely connected words such as we see here:

𝕀 = *the Lo: H: Howard*

The colons above are not meant to represent "and" but rather to abbreviate "Lord" and "Henry."

However, in a couple of cases on the MQS codex sheets, the X was shown to mean the word "and," making line six possibly read, "So, the Earl of Arundel <u>and</u> Lord Henry Howard will." These minor questions do not overshadow the fact that the name of Thomas Howard, Earl of Arundel, the Scottish Master of Masons from possibly about 1630 to 1639, appears twice on the 90' Stone, if the MQS codex is used to translate it.

At first, this struck me as odd – the Howard name never previously having been associated with Oak Island. However, when I learned of the connection of Howard to my overall theory, I had to sit up and take notice, especially with the three uses of the three dot triangle meaning "Scottish Master of Masons."

I have quoted in the past from the 800-page book by Marsha Keith Shuchard entitled *Restoring the Temple of Vision*, which typically sells for $250 or more. This book deals with the idea that many secret societies in western Europe were developed from cabalistic Jewish belief systems, especially in regard to nurturing the Art of Memory and using visualization techniques.

We've heard of a person being called a "visionary" or "he was a man of vision" – phrases similar to this.

Techniques used by some secret societies involved building a better memory by using methods such as creating a "room" or "temple" within the heart or brain where symbols or objects could be placed, representing a certain thing, person or idea that was important to remember. This was loosely called the Art of Memory.

While there were plays and poetry being written, and paintings being painted, the typical man at the top of society seemed to be more focused on architecture. Studies were made in other countries in order to gather ideas and, in addition to notes and drawings being made, a lot of techniques were committed to memory so that, as plans for a new building were being drawn up, these memories could be called upon to create a visualization of the final structure.

Stonemasons had been doing these types of things for centuries, seldom writing down any of their techniques in an effort to keep them secret so that others outside the Masonic guilds could not build such grand structures. This was the basis for Masonic secrecy and included the Mason's Word, secret handshakes and secret symbols along with the Mason's Mark.

When I first discovered that Thomas Howard, Earl of Arundel's name might appear on the 90' Stone when the MQS codex was used to decipher it, I had no idea he had anything to do with Freemasonry. As I gave my 2021 presentation to the Oak Island team in the War Room, I somewhat passed over the three dot triangle symbol.

Later, in *Restoring the Temple of Vision*, I found that: "In November 1618, King James named Sir Francis Bacon, William Herbert, Earl of Pembroke, and Thomas Howard, Earl of Arundel, to a commission on buildings, and he encouraged Inigo Jones to expand his architectural agenda. According to Anderson (here she refers to James Anderson who wrote the book *Constitutions of the Free-Masons*; London, 1723, the first official history of the fraternity), the king approved the Masons' choice of Pembroke as Grand Master in December. Pembroke in turn appointed Jones as his Deputy Grand Master."

Elsewhere, Marsha Shuchard states: "Also staying in Edinburgh Castle were three English nobles who shared King James's architectural ambitions for his southern kingdom. William Herbert, First Earl of Pembroke, had been appointed by James to his building commissions, and he employed Inigo Jones for private work. Also serving on the building commissions and patronizing Jones was Thomas Howard, Earl of Arundel, whose erudite study of architecture included the technical elements involved in quarrying and hewing stones; he was said to love stone so much that he fondled it."

By 1633, according to James Anderson "Thomas Howard, Earl of Arundel, served as Grand Master of the Freemasons with Inigo Jones as his deputy." Also, the book *Historie de la Franc-Maconnerie* (History of French Freemasons) names Howard as Grand Master of the Freemasons in 1635. Significantly, his name was mentioned directly after the name of Al Strachan in this Masonic book.

In 1625, the Earl of Pembroke relinquished the title Scottish Master of Masons to King Charles I, and it was eventually given to Thomas Howard. The French Masonry book states that Howard was followed as the Scottish Master in 1639 by Henry Alexander, the son and heir of William Alexander, and the world's seventh Freemason. Two years later Henry's brother John returned to the area that became New Ross, Nova Scotia, (near Oak Island) where the family lived until 1654.

Howard may have been the Scottish Master by 1632, which has long been my target year for the Money Pit mystery to begin, based on other historical data. He definitely would have been the Master of Masons when William Alexander's sons and Al Strachan became the world's first-recorded non-operative Masons in 1634.

The man (James Anderson) who wrote the very first official history of Freemasonry, plus the men who wrote the history of French Freemasonry (J.A. Faucher and A. Ricker), and the woman (Marsh Keith Shuchard) who wrote an 800-page book on the subject as well, all point to Thomas Howard as the Scottish Master of Masons.

Perhaps significant, a man named James Anderson, one of the earliest lot owners on Oak Island, was also a member of a Masonic Lodge in Nova Scotia.

Possibilities are beginning to mount for the likelihood of Howard's name appearing on the 90' Stone when the MQS codex is used to translate it. The next bit of information from Shuchard's book really points to the 90' Stone being somehow connected to Freemasonry and specifically to Thomas Howard, Earl of Arundel.

Robert Fludd was a doctor in London who, along with Sir Francis Bacon, has been said to have been a member of the Rosicrucians. What would be odd about this is that Fludd preached a mystical answer to most things, as opposed to science, whereas Bacon is often thought of as the godfather of modern science.

Shuchard writes about Fludd that "Demonstrating the mystery of the world's creation 'by way of an arithmetical progression,' he utilized emblematic triangles composed of numbered dots that revealed 'the manner of the world's Fabrick.' These triangles seem to foreshadow the Écossais Masons signature of a triangle composed of three dots."

A triangle composed of three dots! Here, at last, was the clue that solved this symbol on the 90' Stone.

During my MQS translation of the 90' Stone I could not find the triangle made of three dots anywhere on Mary's codex sheets. Now, taking into consideration the Shuchard quote above, the three dot triangle represented the Écossais Masons signature.

Écossais is the French word for Scottish. A popular dictionary website of Freemasonry terms states: "This is a French word, pronounced *a-ko-say*, which Masonically is generally to be translated as Scottish Master."

A Freemason friend of mine confirmed the three dot triangle as an often used Masonic symbol and referred me to several public domain examples of its use.

So, in returning to line eight of the 90' Stone, we can translate it as "Support the Earl of Arundel, God, the Scottish Master of Masons, and Henry Howard."

Thomas Howard, according to several historians, was absolutely the Scottish Master of Masons by 1633.

Another translation for line eight might be "Support Thomas Howard, the Earl of Arundel, God, (*as*) the (*new*) Scottish Master of Masons." This could mean the 90' Stone was a prayer to support Howard in becoming the new Scottish Master of Masons the following year which, in fact, he was. Here's a review of other important points concerning Thomas Howard:

•Thomas Howard's grandfather was on the panel to convict Mary, Queen of Scots, even though he secretly supported her. When he was arrested, pages containing the MQS codex were found hidden under his floor tile.

•Thomas Howard, Earl of Arundel's name is found on a map published in a book from 1624 (the same year the biography of MQS was published). This map was created by William Alexander, whose name has appeared throughout my Oak Island theory, and who has been mentioned by a handful of other Oak Island theorists and authors.

•Sir Francis Bacon died at Thomas Howard's home.

•King James, who gave Nova Scotia to Sir William Alexander, was the godfather of Henry Howard, son of Thomas Howard, whose name also appears on the 90' Stone using the MQS codex.

•Thomas Howard, Sir Francis Bacon and Sir William Alexander were all involved in the Plymouth Company, have all been connected to Shakespeare, and all lived near a place called Charing Cross in London, similar to the old, mysterious name for New Ross, Nova Scotia.

William Alexander and Thomas Howard also served on the Council for Fishing, which began immediately after the expulsion of the Scots from Nova Scotia in 1632. I'll have more on this organization in a future chapter.

It should also be noted that Thomas Howard's son, Henry, was no shrinking violet and followed his father as 3rd Earl of Arundel. Henry was formally trained in symbolic Heraldry, and was the proprietor of Carolana, which was established south of the Virginia Colony, and which became the Carolinas as we know them today.

While still in his twenties, Henry became involved in overseas activities that rivaled those of his father. In 1632, he was accepted on the Council for New England and, along with others, received grants of territory from that body. One 17th century observer stated that this "Son and heir to the Lord Arundel had a wonderful inclination and a great sagacity in promoting the plantation of Northern America and some of the islands thereunto adjacent." Could Lord Henry Howard actually be the man who created the 90′ Stone?

Although I can't yet fully explain this stone's message, here is my complete paraphrased translation of the 90′ Stone, using the Mary, Queen of Scots, codex:

O, God send Angels, and send support to Edinburgh, Scotland. Send Edinburgh the great treasure and the Scottish Master of Masons. Support Thomas Howard, Earl of Arundel, God, as the Scottish Master of Masons, and his son Lord Henry Howard.

Thomas Howard was connected to William Alexander in many ways and was one of the largest collectors of manuscripts, paintings, jewelry and other fine pieces, in English history. His most complete biography states: "As an early collector, and especially as an intermediary for collectors of larger means than he himself possessed, he deserves a distinct niche in the temple of fame."

The same biography also states: "In January 1632, Lord Arundel appointed Sir Henry Bourchier to act as his deputy in the Court Military, in the case between Lord Reay and David Ramsay; which suggests that he was about to undertake an absence of some duration or distance. No further clue has been found to throw light on wither he was bound, or what the object."

Howard made a mysterious and as yet unexplained trip for some "duration or distance" beginning two months before the Scots were expelled from Nova Scotia, the exact year I've pinpointed for the Money Pit mystery to begin. The hearing he was to preside over involved David Ramsay, occultist, official clock-maker for the king, and Freemason who, according to the book *Restoring the Temple of Vision*, was the man who followed William Alexander as the magistrate of a new Templar/Masonic organization which became the Freemasons.

David Ramsay began the long-standing leadership that the Ramsay family has held within Freemasonry right up to the current day under William "Ramsay" McGhee. The Ramsay family also established Dalhousie University, located just one hour from Oak Island, and four Ramsays became Knights Baronet of Nova Scotia.

Thomas Howard is recorded as the Scottish Master of Masonry "by 1633," and may have been the Scottish Master as early as 1632. A few years earlier he had been appointed to a building committee for King Charles and had spent considerable time in Edinburgh along with an earlier Grand Master of Masons, the Earl of Pembroke.

In 1634, William Alexander's sons, William Jr. and Anthony, along with his partner Al Strachan, became the world's earliest recorded non-operative Masons under Grand Master Howard, or what we know today as the Freemasons. David Ramsay followed shortly thereafter.

That Thomas Howard, Earl of Arundel, was associated with the beginnings of Freemasonry and could have traveled to Oak Island in early 1632 (and perhaps buried some collectibles, including works by Sir Francis Bacon, who died in Howard's house) is entirely possible based on the most detailed biography of his life. This could be the very clue that proponents of the Baconian theory of the Money Pit have been looking for – basically how and when Bacon's papers were transported to Oak Island.

This doesn't discount the idea that additional treasure gained through Alexander Strachan's robbery of the Keith fortune, and possible clan collectibles from the days of the Knights Templar, were also buried in the same depository until such time as the volatile situation in Europe settled down. That just never happened.

Both Sir William Alexander and Thomas Howard, Earl of Arundel, expressed wishes of escaping the troubles of Europe to find a remote place to hide away – in Howard's case "on an island sea-girt," or surrounded by water.

The names of these men appear on the 90′ Stone when the MQS codex is used. ABOVE: Thomas Howard, Earl of Arundel and Scottish Master of Masons from some time after 1630 until 1639. BELOW: Thomas's son, Lord Henry Howard.

Chapter Six

THE MARK OF FOUR

The thought of Neanderthals playing Tic-Tac-Toe seems a bit hilarious... but...

Below is a photograph of a crosshatch design found in Gorham's Cave in Gibraltar that was taken by Stewart Finlayson. The cave was explored by archeologists Clive and Stewart Finlayson, along with other local historians. The photo is of cave art traced to Neanderthal people from around 30,000 years ago and it appears eerily similar to the 3x3 grid of Tic-Tac-Toe shown next to it.

No one is suggesting Neanderthals played Tic-Tac-Toe. An associate of the Finlaysons, Francesco d'Errico, director of research at the French Centre National de la Recherche Scientifique, states: "It does not necessarily mean that it is symbolic - in the sense that it represents something else – but it was done on purpose."

The archaeologists estimate that the full engraving would have required 200-300 strokes with a stone cutting tool, taking at least an hour to create.

As Clive Finlayson explained: "One intriguing aspect is that the engraving is at the point in the cave where the cave's orientation changes by 90 degrees."

After examining dozens of Ice Age caves across Europe, another paleoarchaeologist, Genevieve von Petzinger, discovered our ancestors repeatedly used 32 symbols or signs. She tells us: "There was something about them that I found much more interesting than the (drawings of) animals and (of) the people. Those are nice too, but it seemed like there were some patterns going on there, and yet there was not enough information to even delve into it."

Petzinger set out to document and systematically catalogue the geometric signs that were created tens of thousands of years ago in Europe during the Ice Age.

She started by compiling a database of the geometric signs found at the nearly 370 known rock art sites across the continent. From these sites, and by exploring some rarely documented sites, she was able to isolate many commonly used symbols.

Paleoanthropologists had long believed that art was invented during a "creative explosion" 40,000 years ago in Europe — the first Homo sapiens are thought to have migrated there from Africa during an Ice Age warm spell roughly 45,000 years ago.

But Genevieve von Petzinger's research challenges this conventional wisdom.

"I realized that two-thirds of the signs were already in use when humans arrived in Europe," she says, suggesting the symbols are a continuation of an existing tradition stretching back to the Neanderthals rather than the start of something new by humans.

Below are the 32 common symbols found in hundreds of prehistoric caves and catalogued by Petzinger.

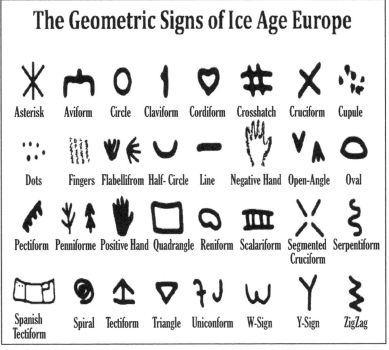

Petzinger believes these cave symbols were the very root of alphabetical systems that later developed, and that the symbols were a quick way to explain or identify a thought, person, place or thing.

It seems the idea of a simple symbol representing a complete word or even a complete thought was not new in the time of Mary, Queen of Scots.

In fact, most early languages used symbols, not words, to convey thoughts, as shown for example on the Egyptian carved-stone tablet (see page 23). Today, we have international symbols, our smart phone emojis, company logos, and compasses on maps all meant to represent a deeper meaning than a few letters could.

The same is true for flags and for Heraldry, where an overall symbol made up of smaller symbols is meant to convey the heritage and history of a country or family. Simpler versions of these kinds of symbols were also used to represent lesser families and individuals. They were a common man's coat of arms, in a sense.

The use of symbols to convey words and ideas can be found in Egyptian hieroglyphics, Sumerian, Aztec, Inca, Mayan and some Asian languages, plus coats of arms, religious symbols and even modern hazard symbols. During the time of the Underground Railroad there were the so-called "quilt codes," and during the heyday of the American tramp there were the "hobo codes."

Using symbols rather than single letters to convey a message has been perhaps the rule throughout human history. We know that Masons had used certain types of marks to sign their stonework. It was a practical issue for them as they wanted to make sure they got paid for each stone they worked, and they wanted inferior stones to be easily identified by their stonemason's marks.

We should also not be surprised that merchants in the British Isles and elsewhere were using symbols (like the one found on the Oak Island bag or bale seal) to identify their products, companies and workmen.

"Sign of Four" bag seal found on Oak Island.

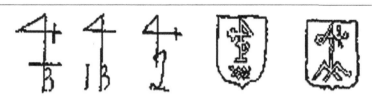

ENGLISH MERCHANT ADVENTURES MARKS

MASONS MARKS SCOTLAND   ENGLAND

From a centuries-old book on merchant and mason marks we have the above illustrations. One thing these examples have in common is that they all use what is known as the Mark of Four, or the Sign of Four.

In fact, I've found that virtually all early merchant adventurers, especially those involved with settlements in the New World, used a Mark of Four similar to the one shown on the Oak Island bag seal. This symbol was apparently thought to ward off the devil since overseas travel and settlement was a risky business in the 1600s and 1700s.

But why this symbol?

There are two existing theories that take a look at the Mark of Four as being a religious symbol.

One is that it is the pattern that is believed to represent the sign of the cross that some people use while praying. Others believe it might be the mirror image of the early Christian symbol for Christ called the Chi Rho. This so-called "labarum" is a christogram, shown in the illustration below, formed from the first two Greek letters of the word "Christ."

When the symbol is flipped, the P faces left similar to the top of the cross found on Oak Island. It also becomes closer to the Mark of Four symbol.

Below are several merchant marks using the Mark of Four design. Number 24 looks identical to the mark found on the bag or bale seal discovered on Oak Island except for the two letters. It has been loosely connected to Norwich, England, where the wool trade flourished.

Michael Drayton, a poet and playwright of the time, commented on this. Wool made England rich and the staple port of Norwich "in her state doth stand with towns of highest regard, the fourth of all the land," as Drayton noted in 1612.

We can't be sure that the Oak Island seal came from Norwich wool, as the description of the #24 symbol is vague at best. However, other identical symbols were found in and around Norwich, not just on lead seals but also on wood workings, metal workings and more.

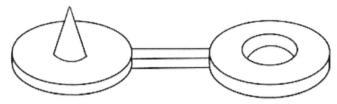

The lead bag or bale seal was a simple contraption. A pin on the left side was fed through the fabric so as not to damage it and was placed in the hole on the right side of the seal. This was then crimped together in an operation that not only made it seem like a one piece flat seal, but also embedded the merchant's trademark into the lead. The letters found on either side of the Oak Island Mark of Four seal are said to belong to the craftsman who made or dyed the cloth, the inspector of the cloth, or the merchant who sold the cloth.

Four dissimilar bale seals were found at one archaeological site lying uniformly next to each other indicating that they had all been attached to the same item. Perhaps this item had these seals attached to it to represent different stages of processing.

Stonemasons had been making their marks on stones for years. Others were casting their unique marks in wax seals, including some Knights Templar.

Title deeds and important documents often had wax seals attached. A perfect example is the 1320 Declaration of Arbroath shown below, which carries the seals of some of the most famous families in all of Scotland.

In my own theory of Oak Island, one of the items on the list of treasures stolen by Al Strachan was a seal bag that held the deeds to a few castles. These bags were made of canvas and waterproofed three times in candle wax, explaining how a small bit of parchment could have been pulled up from the Money Pit that had been flooded for decades and yet its ink was not smeared.

There is also a note entitled "Handwriting of Dan Blankenship" found in author D'Arcy O'Conner's Oak Island research which identifies a wax seal found on Oak Island. A very interesting section reads: "Western Geophysical President Vinnie Murphy recovered (a) wax seal (in the) design of (a) HEART, similar to that found in Haiti, on O.I."

Vincent "Vinnie" Murphy carried out a review of the Oak Island Barringer survey in 1989. Perhaps there is more info on this in Dan's records or elsewhere.

In the case of my theory, wax seals would have accompanied title deeds to castles, such as those stolen by Al Strachan. The Strachans had their own seal, that of a Highland stag, a symbol also found stamped on silverware taken from a shipwreck found within sight of Oak Island.

It is quite obvious that symbols, rather than individual letters, can relate a much larger story. It may have been a mistake right from the beginning to assume that the symbols on the 90' Stone were meant to facilitate a simple letter substitution code rather than a symbol-for-word substitution.

If so, the MQS code fills the bill in providing a word for every symbol on the 90' Stone. No other code or translation in the history of the stone has ever been able to do that. Obviously, the symbols for Thomas Howard, Scottish Master of Masons, and his son Henry, being found on the 90' Stone (if based on the Mary, Queen of Scots, ciphers) presents a whole new area of needed research and explanation.

Chapter Seven

THE COUNCIL ON FISHING

What if the 90' Stone is a very important clue as to what was buried in the Money Pit, who buried it, and why – the ultimate X that marks the spot?

What if the 90' Stone actually is a cipher based on the codex of Mary, Queen of Scots, featuring the words "Great Treasure," "Edinburgh, Scotland," "O, God Send Angels," plus the names of a father and son team – Thomas Howard, Earl of Arundel and Scottish Master of Masons, and his son Henry Howard, who was much engaged in the settlement of the New World?

As I finished my 2021 presentation for the Oak Island team on the MQS code, I was reasonably sure I had turned over every leaf in connecting Thomas Howard, Earl of Arundel, to William Alexander, Francis Bacon, Kings James and Charles, and Nova Scotia. I should know by now that the clues and research never end for someone afflicted with "Islanditis."

While poking around in an old book on a different subject I found a very interesting obscure bit of text. It mentioned an organization that was established on July 19, 1632, under the title of "The Council and Committee of the Fishing of his Majesty's Dominions of Great Britain and Ireland."

Fishing vessels have been used throughout history to spy on an enemy. For example, the U.S.S.R. used them within 70 miles of the Delaware coast during the Cold War. I immediately wondered if this could be the case here, since this council began only one month after most of the Scots fled Nova Scotia. Plus, there were around 50 Scots left behind who still needed to be rescued.

The council consisted of twelve men, six Scotsmen and six Englishmen. They held their position for life unless removed for good cause. Though King Charles I didn't create the council he still regarded it with great favor, considering it to be of national importance.

Within the Scottish half of the council was William Alexander; within the English half was Thomas Howard, whose name appears on the 90' Stone if the MQS code is used. Both men held land near the original bounds of Nova Scotia, Howard's name is found on Alexander's 1624 map of Nova Scotia, and both men were significant in the very beginnings of Freemasonry.

Once again, it seems very coincidental that two men who could be part of my Oak Island theory from 1632 also happened, in the exact same year, to appear together as members of this important council. If nothing else, this record proves they knew each other well and in the exact year of my theory. July 1632 would be one month after the time period that I've proposed (since 2017) for the creation of the Money Pit (April, May and June 1632), plus just six months after Howard's mysterious disappearance, and five months before the creation of the *Grand Lodge Manuscript* of Masonry *(see page 115).*

My theory is based on the order for the Scots to leave Port Royal, Nova Scotia, in March 1632, and a letter from June 1632, written by Alexander, acknowledging that his people had been driven out by the French. Forming a Fishing Committee and Council in the following month would provide the perfect cover for going back to Nova Scotia under the guise of patrolling the fishing waters there, noted for their abundance of fish long before the Scots or even the French ever got to Port Royal.

Beyond the twelve person council there were an additional 136 assistants, mostly lawyers, lords and knights, allowing for almost any eventuality.

The question I now had was – If William Alexander and Thomas Howard had a stake in the Council because of Oak Island, what connection or benefit would the other ten council members realize, or expect to realize?

So I began investigating every single member of the fishing committee. William Alexander and Thomas Howard represented Scotland and England respectively and we have at least some idea of how they are connected to Oak Island.

The remaining five Scots:

•**William, Earl of Morton,** was actually Sir William Douglas. On March 28, 1604, he married Lady Anne Keith, a daughter of George Keith, 5th Earl Marischal. He was implicated in the robbery of his father-in-law, George Keith, which was orchestrated by Al Strachan. He also became one of the first Knights Baronet of Nova Scotia. William Douglas, Earl of Morton, went on to become the Treasurer of Scotland from 1630 to 1636.

• **Robert, Earl of Roxburgh**, or Robert Ker/Kerr, was a cousin to Andrew Kerr, Knight Baronet of Nova Scotia. After his second wife's death in 1643, Robert married Lady Isobel Douglas, fifth daughter of the previously mentioned William Douglas by his wife, Lady Anne Keith, eldest daughter of Earl Marischal George Keith.

Robert Ker's last will and testament mentions a "portrait of Anne of Denmark (wife of James I), set with diamonds." As previously shown, Robert Ker's father-in-law, William Douglas, was a co-conspirator in the Keith robbery and one of the first Knights Baronet.

A significant item on the long list of treasure stolen by Al Strachan and William Douglas (from George Keith) was "the Queen of Denmark's picture in gold, set about with rich diamonds, estimated at 5000 merks." The diamond encrusted picture of Anne, Queen of Denmark, and wife of James I, seems to appear both on the Al Strachan stolen treasure list and in Robert Ker's will.

• **John Hay, Esq.,** was the grand uncle of the first Hay Baronet, one James Hay, the personal lawyer for King James I (who gave Nova Scotia to William Alexander, and who chartered the Knights Baronet). Three additional men surnamed Hay also became Knights Baronet of Nova Scotia.

• **William, Earl of Strathern**, was actually William Graham, Knight Baronet of Nova Scotia. He renounced his lands and title of Earl of Strathern to King Charles I, on January 22, 1630 (more likely 1631, based on old vs. new calendar dating practices). Witnessing this act were four additional Knights Baronet of Nova Scotia.

They were Sir Colin Campbell, Sir William Maxwell, Sir James Gordon and Sir Thomas Hope (coincidentally, a forefather to Joan Hope who owned and discovered the New Ross foundation). William Graham was reconfirmed in his Strathern lands and title on July 31, 1631, and one year later was made a member of the Fishing Council.

•**George Fletcher, Esq.,** was a "Gentleman of the Privy Chamber in Ordinary" to King Charles I. Those who held this position were noble-born servants to the crown who would wait and attend the king in private, as well as during various court activities and functions. George was born about 1605. He was also known as Sir George Fletcher of Restenneth, a priory in Angushsire, Scotland, owned by the Erskine family of William Alexander's wife, and also of John Erskine who wrote William Alexander's charter for Nova Scotia.

This does it for the six Scots on the Council (including William Alexander) all of whom are connected somehow to the Knights Baronet of Nova Scotia, with two of them directly connected to the robbery of George Keith by Al Strachan. Seems pretty suspicious, or at least convenient, if the goal was to keep an eye on Oak Island.

The five remaining Brits:

•**Sir John Cooke/Cook/Coke** appears several times in official State Papers as Chief Justice of Ireland although he was British himself. He later led the prosecution of Charles I before the king's beheading. After the Restoration of Charles II, John Cooke was hanged, drawn and quartered.

From "The House of Names" website - "John Cooke (or John Cook, John Coke, 1608-1660), was the first Solicitor General of the English Commonwealth and led the prosecution of Charles I." John descended from an earlier Sir John Cooke, also a lawyer, through his son Anthony. And, surprisingly, Anthony's daughter Anne Cooke was married to Sir Nicholas Bacon, and was the mother of Sir Francis Bacon!

Sir John Cooke's father, William, was the brother of Anne, so Sir John Cooke would be the first cousin of Sir Francis Bacon. Also connecting these men is an entry in the *State Papers*, 1608, Jan 31: "Grant at the suit of Sir Francis Bacon to Sir William Cooke Sr. of the king's reversion of the estates in Hert" (estates left to Sir Francis by his parents Nicholas and Anne neé Cooke Bacon).

•**Richard, Lord Weston,** was the Chancellor of the Exchequer and later Lord Treasurer of England (in 1628, the year William Alexander's first settlers left for Nova Scotia). He was one of the most influential figures in the early years of Charles I. Weston was a patron of Ben Johnson, a contemporary of Shakespeare. An obscure record from 1547 shows a Will'us Sheldon de Weston as a patron of Roger Shadspere. How these two men from 1547 relate to the later Richard Weston and the famous author William Shakespeare is not yet understood.

•**Philip, Earl of Pembroke**, was Lord Steward of the Household for Charles I. He and his older brother William (one-time Scottish Master of Masons) were the "incomparable pair of brethren" to whom the First Folio of Shakespeare's collected works was dedicated (1623).

•**Thomas, Viscount Savage,** was appointed the Commissioner of Trade in 1626; the Commissioner to advise as to ways and means of increasing the King's revenue in July 1626, and also for the sale of the King's lands on September 15, 1626. Savage's forefather, John Savage, was one of the Catholic conspirators in the plot to kill Queen Elizabeth and put the Catholic Mary, Queen of Scots, on the throne. Savage was to be the person who would personally assassinate Elizabeth. He was violently executed along with his co-conspirators.

•**Francis, Lord Cottington,** was made a privy councillor on November 12, 1628, and, in March 1629, was appointed Chancellor of the Exchequer and head of the Treasury. He and Francis Bacon were on opposing sides when Parliament was dissolved in 1614. As Clerk of the Council, Cottingham burned all the "notes, arguments, and collections" of the defunk Parliament, while Sir Francis Bacon had been among the most vocal in favor of calling the Parliament in the first place.

This is stunning information about an organization founded just one month after the Knights Baronet settlers finally left Nova Scotia. The Council was nearly lopsided with leaders associated with the Knights Baronet of Nova Scotia, and with men high in the government of King Charles. Two men were directly associated with Mary, Queen of Scots, through their forefathers (Howard and Savage), two were associated with the robbery of George Keith (Douglas and Ker), and four were associated with Sir Francis Bacon (Howard, Cooke, Cottington and Alexander).

In addition, among the 136 assistants to the Fishing Council was Lord Henry Howard whose name may also appear on the 90' Stone, as well as others who were or had Knights Baronet within their families.

While this group would certainly have had its hands full, if regulating the important trade of fishing within Great Britain proper, their heavy influence from the Knights Baronet of Nova Scotia could well have led them to send spies to that province in fishing boats. After all, their people had been fishing there even before William Alexander received and named Nova Scotia.

Information, beyond a few statements of their assumed responsibilities, is rare for this Council. It is known that William Alexander was still a member by at least 1636, and that the original group is thought to have dissolved as the War of Three Kingdoms, the civil war of Great Britain, got underway.

There is strong evidence that William Alexander had intentions of becoming King (or at least de facto king) of Nova Scotia with 100-150 knights serving him. I think there is a chance that he originally saw the Council on Fishing as a new source of followers, or possibly spies, once his Nova Scotia venture stalled out.

Within two years he may have chosen stonemasons of Scotland as an additional bulwark, having his two sons and partner initiated as the world's first-known non-operative (or not actively working) Masons in history, with his friend Thomas Howard serving as Scottish Grand Master of the Masons (without any doubt) during the year of their initiations – 1634.

Before delving deeply into Masonic history there is one important point that needs to be made. The *Old Charges of British Freemasonry*, a book written by William Hughan, in 1872, describes a scroll called the *Grand Lodge Manuscript*. Though initially thought to date to December 25, 1132, the author makes the case that the date actually reads "December 25, 1632," and that the second "1" in the date was simply poorly written. Upon further inspection, it was shown to be a "6" and he adds, "as that is about the period when it was written."

While the *Grand Lodge Manuscript* gives a Biblical origin to stonemasonry, it is focused on two principal instructions - remaining true to God and King, and remaining respectable, as to not bring shame on the pragmatic craft of stonemasonry. There is no mention of degrees, of esoteric beliefs or of symbolic rituals, as are often associated with Freemasonry. It seems to be a practical guide to maintaining a career in stonemasonry, rather than any type of mystical or esoteric presentation of Masonic beliefs.

The date 1632 caught my eye as that is the year I have proposed that future Freemasons put in motion activities that resulted in the burial of a treasure on Oak Island.

Two years later, William Alexander, Jr., Anthony Alexander and Alexander Strachan became the first three recorded non-operative Masons. Within another three years, a Stewart cousin of the King became the fourth, David Ramsay became the fifth, with possibly Sir William Alexander as the sixth. The seventh was Henry Alexander, Scottish Master of Masons as of 1639.

These records still exist and shortly after the first three initiations, the word Freemason (spelled "Frie Mesones") is used for the first time in a Scottish Lodge.

Just about this time, honorary or non-operative Freemasons began to incorporate esoteric beliefs into Masonic Lodges being led by William Alexander and David Ramsay, two known fans of Rosicrucianism and esoteric beliefs, especially Jewish cabalistic beliefs.

There are no alternative records to what I have presented here, and if there are, I would love to see them.

The fact that the *Grand Lodge Manuscript* book was published in 1632, the same year the Scots left Nova Scotia, and the same year the Council on Fishing was created, is of great interest. Add to this the fact that Thomas Howard, a member of the Council on Fishing, was almost certainly the Scottish Master of Masons by 1630, and it might not seem so strange that his name appears on the 90' Stone from the Oak Island Money Pit right next to the Masonic symbol for "Scottish Master," when the codex of Mary, Queen of Scots, is used to translate it.

Thomas Howard was connected to William Alexander, to Sir Francis Bacon (who died in his home), and to Shakespeare. His mysterious disappearance in January 1632, his position as the Scottish Master of Masons, and the connections of his ancestors to Mary, Queen of Scots, all make his name appearing twice on the 90' Stone become a possibility worth serious consideration and much further research.

Chapter Eight
FREEMASONRY BEGINS

William Alexander, founder of Nova Scotia, was one of the most influential men in creating what is now known as the Freemasons.

Alexander was a powerful man in both Scottish and English government, having been a friend of James VI of Scotland when he took over as King James I of England and Ireland as well. He was also the childhood tutor of Prince Charles, who followed his father as Charles I.

Both James I and his son Charles I were supportive of Alexander's adventure in Nova Scotia, and of his formation of the Knights Baronet of Nova Scotia in an attempt to gain financing and settlers for his new colony. This colony called Nova Scotia (New Scotland in Latin) was actually meant to serve as a buffer between French Canada and the settlers at Plymouth, Massachusetts.

Alexander was also closely associated with a man named William Vaughan, who had a similar, speculative colony in Newfoundland.

A 1910 *Americana* story on the Knights Baronet states, "As a direct result of the publicity campaign conducted by William Alexander, Robert Gordon and Dr. William Vaughan, and the creation of the Knights Baronet, the enterprise (Nova Scotia) received a new impetus."

Yet, even before the Knights Baronet were formed, Alexander's men and possibly he, himself, were carrying out secretive undertakings in Nova Scotia. In 1624, Alexander wrote: "I have never remembered anything with more admiration than America." While there is no official record of Alexander being in America, in order to remember something, you have to have experienced it!

It has been speculated that a year earlier Alexander had a secret estate built along Gold River, about 17 miles inland from Oak Island, in a spot where the French, who were still stationed at Port Royal (on the opposite side of Nova Scotia), could be spied on and eventually attacked. I wrote an entire book on this subject entitled *Oak Island And New Ross*, and I would direct you there for all the tremendous number of details I've discovered.

One other note worth mentioning here is that, in 1626, King Charles I noted: "A place in America commonly called by the name of Nova Scotia, already discovered and surveyed by the pains and travel of our well-beloved counsellor, Sir William Alexander of Menstrie." (Note: Menstrie Castle was Alexander's home in Scotland).

We have both King Charles I and William Alexander indicating that, in fact, Alexander had visited Nova Scotia. The only year this could have happened was in 1623 when the secret estate was said to have been built according to Alexander family and Mi'kmaq legends.

There are two very interesting letters found in the papers of King James I that refer to William Alexander and his need for money and secrecy in the Nova Scotia adventure. We'll look at these next.

Below, I list the date of each letter and their general contents as described in the list:

•January 23, 1624 – *Letter from Secretary of State Edward Conway to the Lord Treasurer Lionel Cranfield, 1st Earl of Middlesex, to provide money for Sir William Alexander, who is to be employed in the King's special service* (typically meaning military intelligence).

•February 4, 1624 – *Sir William Alexander to Sec. Conway. Fears the Lord Treasurer's delay in his dispatch will sacrifice substance to form, and discover* (or reveal) *the business. Suggests that* (Philip) *Burlamachi* (the king's financier) *might furnish him privately and quietly with money, by selling some iron ordnance* (sic) *which he is allowed to transport. Fears the business is too much divulged, but hopes it may be managed so as to avoid disgrace, should it fail.*

The effort in Nova Scotia would, in fact, be a special service or military/intelligence operation: spying on the French to determine their strength, and preparing for the battle that would oust them from Port Royal.

The expeditions of 1622 and 1623 did not pass without comment from the French government as well. In spring 1624, the Comte de Tillieres, French ambassador to England, addressed a strong "remonstrance" to the British government over English hostilities in Canada.

Further revealing his financial needs, Sir William wrote to one of his associates: "I can lift no monie here in hast(e); the English marchants never taking Scottish securitie, and the Scottish factours not haveing monie."

The fact that behind-the-scenes military and financial moves were being made by William Alexander, with the approval of the king, is without question. His Knights Baronet order was created specifically to provide both money and manpower to create a British colony in Nova Scotia and I feel, based on a lot of evidence, to install himself as King of Nova Scotia.

The first batch of Knights Baronet were all somehow connected to the robbery of George Keith by Strachan. This is a matter of official record. It appears the theft was either premeditated by all concerned or William Alexander simply decided to take advantage of Al Strachan's position as an indicted rich man. It was in his 1624 book that Sir William writes of a man named Villegagnon (vil-ga-non), the very man who spirited the child Mary, Queen of Scots, out of Scotland:

He had a desire to retire himself from the vanity, corruption, and vexation of their parts to some remote place in America, where he might, free from all kind of impediments, begin a new life, and where he hoped to found such a Colony as should serve for a retreat to where all those weary of the persecutions at home could go where they might live with safety, and enjoy the liberty of their conscience.

Oddly, a similar statement was made about Thomas Howard whose name appears on Alexander's 1624 map and also possibly on the 90' Stone, if the codex of Mary, Queen of Scots, is used to translate it. Howard had a very detailed, well-respected biography written of his life.

A quote from that book reads, "Throughout his career there runs a curious double thread. On the one side was the 'perfect courtier,' serving his King with unvarying devotion... On the other is found the lover of distant lands and secluded haunts, of islands sea-girt and solitary, where a man might hide from the world, and live a life of freedom, far from the conventional demands and distractions of society."

With all the intrigue and religious persecution taking place around this time in European history, it may not be that surprising to find that three very significant men, Alexander, Villegagnon and Howard, all wished to find a new secret home and to make a fresh start in America. Villegagnon still has an island named for him in Brazil.

This could be the actual era in which Freemasonry took a special interest in helping establish a new world order, a utopia of a people who were free of the limitations of the past, to be located in America.

At one point there also arose a connection of William Alexander to the Vaughan name when William Vaughan, who was mentioned in the 1910 *Americana* article, came to visit Charles I, as a supporter of the Rosicrucians.

Author Marsha Keith Schuchard, in her book *Restoring the Temple of Vision*, writes: "It is possible that Alexander and Vaughan were aware of a real Rosicrucian (Philip Zeigler) who was then resident in London. Moreover, it was David Ramsay who acted as intermediary between the mysterious visitor (Zeigler) and the court."

David Ramsay was another one of the earliest non-operative initiates into the Edinburgh Masonic Lodge.

Schuchard writes that Ramsay followed William Alexander as "acting magistrate" of a secret Templar-Masonic Order, presumed to be Freemasons. Another interesting point about David Ramsay is that he was a practitioner of the occult, having both a philosopher's stone and a dowsing rod.

I've written in past books about how the Ramsay family has played a major role in leading Scottish Freemasonry all the way up to the present day. They also founded Dalhousie University located just an hour from Oak Island, which has been connected to the search on the island in the past.

Rick Lagina, Doug Crowell and I had been scheduled to meet with the archivist of Dalhousie University for a couple of months. When I arrived for my War Room meeting that year, Doug announced that Dalhousie University had cancelled the meeting at the last minute with no reason given. It has remained a mystery as to why our meeting, that had been discussed in several emails over the last few months, was suddenly cancelled.

Sir William Vaughan's cousin Henry, a metaphysical author, wrote an enigmatic line after the beheading of King Charles I that reads, "Thus is the solemn temple sunk again, into a pillar, and concealed from men." One definition for the word pillar is "a shaft," and a shaft is synonymous with a tunnel, passage or pit.

Reviewing a few Vaughan family genealogies I was able to discover the complete connection of William Vaughan, friend of William Alexander, to Anthony Vaughan Jr., one of the discoverers of the Money Pit.

I have, for a long time now, suspected that Anthony Vaughan Jr., of Money Pit fame, was related to William Vaughan, friend to Sir William Alexander, the Scottish proprietor of Nova Scotia, and the man who actually named the province in 1621. I believe I now have the proof which I published in my book *Oak Island And The Mayflower*.

William Vaughan may even have played a role in the creation of the Freemasons, considering it was he who introduced William Alexander to Rosicrucianism.

William Alexander had always been a fan of the ancient histories and myths of Greece and Rome. He was also a man who found it necessary to perpetuate a lot of secrecy in his involvement with Nova Scotia.

David Ramsay (member of the Dalhousie University founding family), according to author Marsha Keith Schuchard, appears to have followed Sir William Alexander as acting magistrate of a secret Templar-Masonic Order. Since there was no such thing as a Freemason before this time, a secret Templar-Masonic Order could simply have meant a new type of Mason who incorporated esoteric teaching into his Masonic life, and this points to the Alexander family, and their Strachan, Ramsay and Howard friends, as most likely creating modern Freemasonry.

William Alexander's sons, William Jr. and Anthony, were accepted as the first known non-operative Masons. Alexander's partner, Al Strachan, was the third. David Ramsay, a close personal aide to King Charles I, and relative of Al Strachan, was initiated a few years later.

Ramsay was sponsored by Alexander's two sons, and by Alexander's partner, Al Strachan. A non-operative Mason was simply an honorary member who did not operate daily as a stonemason. There is no earlier record for a person of this standing before William Alexander Jr. and those who immediately followed him.

This younger William Alexander also led the Scots in Nova Scotia from 1628 through 1632. So this means that, quite significantly, the world's first Freemason was also leader of the Knights Baronet settlers in Nova Scotia.

We can equally be certain that William Alexander's Knights Baronet of Nova Scotia had links back in time to the Knights Templar, and the premier link forward in time to the Freemasons through his own sons, William Jr., the first Freemason, Anthony, the second, and Henry, the seventh (later the Scottish Master, as of 1639).

William Alexander was actually William Alexander MacDonald. He believed this. He had his coat of arms reflect this. He often signed his name this way.

The Alexander family name came from a man named Alexander MacDonald. Clan Donald historians have, for a couple of centuries, argued whether this was Alexander, the brother of Angus Og MacDonald, or Alexander, the son of Angus Og MacDonald.

The point is somewhat moot as, either way, it was Angus Og MacDonald who sheltered the Scottish hero-king Robert the Bruce at his lowest point in his contest against England, and helped him drive the English out of Scotland at the final battle (the famous Battle of Bannockburn).

Angus Og MacDonald, ancestor to William Alexander, is said to have arrived late in the battle with somewhere between 5,000 and 10,000 men, causing the English to turn and run, at least those who weren't already killed.

MacDonald, in some quarters, is said to have been a Knight Templar, and was almost certainly a Crusader Knight. An ancient Crusader's cross was recently found on the island where Angus was buried. These crosses were driven into the ground just before a battle and retrieved if the knight lived. They were of a unique design and appear on most Clan Donald coats of arms, including the arms of William Alexander.

Some historians believe that Robert the Bruce was also a Knight Templar, and most historians at least accept that the Knights Templar took shelter in Scotland because Bruce and his entire country had already been excommunicated.

Other historians have offered the theory that Angus Og MacDonald led the Knights Templar at Bannockburn, and that it was they who made the English turn and run. Something I've discovered, that I've read nowhere else, is that the Bannockburn battle happened 99 days after Jacques de Molay was burned at the stake.

The date given in the chronicle of Guillaume de Nangis, for the death of Jacques de Molay, was the day after the Feast of Saint Gregory, or Monday, March 18, 1314. This is the date most often accepted. The Battle of Bannockburn took place on the 23rd and 24th of June, 1314, the 24th being exactly 99 days after Jacques de Molay's death (counting Molay's death as day one).

The number nine has been extremely significant in secret society lore. There were originally nine Templars. The cabalistic tree of life of the Jews consists of nine branches or worlds. The Freemasons have The Secret Vault that contains the Ninth Arch where the Sacred Treasure was kept. And there were nine levels to the Money Pit before the 90' Stone was found.

Not only did Angus Og MacDonald earn the right for the MacDonalds to always fight at the right hand of the king but also, not long after Bannockburn, the Alexander branch of MacDonalds was given the land at Menstrie where they built the castle that Sir William was later born in. Also born at that castle were William Jr. and Anthony Alexander, the world's first two Freemasons.

William Alexander's ancestor, Gilbert, received land in that area shortly after the Battle of Bannockburn. By the early 1400s, his direct ancestors began being called Lords of Menstrie, holding their land, in various ways, under the oversight of the Campbell clan.

But that's hardly it!

Menstrie Castle is located less than seven miles from the Bannockburn battlefield, and the land it is on is recorded as formerly being Knights Templar land. On file in the Scottish Public Record Office in Edinburgh, Scotland, there is reference to the Alexanders being fully granted the Templar lands at Menstrie in 1537, and again in 1553. The second re-granting of the land in 1553 would have been by Mary, Queen of Scots, who would then be directly responsible for Alexander's home being located on former Templar land.

William Alexander and his sons were descended from Angus Og MacDonald (as is Sir Ian MacDonald MacUisdean, the current premier Knight Baronet of Nova Scotia, as am I), and all these Alexander's were born and raised on this Knights Templar land.

Sir William Alexander MacDonald Jr. and Sir Anthony Alexander MacDonald became the world's first known Freemasons. Can you get any closer of a connection? Can there be any chain of events that better connects the Knights Templar to the Freemasons and, by the way, to the Knights Baronet of Nova Scotia?

I told the story in my *Oak Island Knights* book of how I found a lot of this information, but it's worth retelling again. I've shown the Alexander family's connections to the Knights Templar earlier in this book. Obviously, there could be no men more connected with the Knights Baronet of Nova Scotia than Sir William Sr. who created them, and William Jr. who led them in Nova Scotia.

The final connection comes from the fact that the younger William Alexander also became the world's first Freemason, his brother Anthony became the second, and his brother Henry became the seventh.

I went into the reasons why this happened in my second book, *Oak Island 1632*, but what I didn't have at the time was a copy of the actual document. Thanks to Kel Hancock, Grand Historian of the Grand Lodges of Freemasonry in Nova Scotia, I was led to the book *History of The Lodge of Edinburgh* by David Murray Lyon, Grand Steward of the Grand Lodge of Scotland, written in 1873.

Coincidentally or not, this book was dedicated posthumously to a later Ramsay, Earl of Dalhousie, Grand Master of the Scottish Freemasons, and acting Grand Master of the English Freemasons.

This book reproduced the actual documents from 1634 showing that William Jr. and Anthony Alexander, along with their father's partner Alexander Strachan were the first three men initiated into a stonemason's lodge as non-operative or accepted Masons.

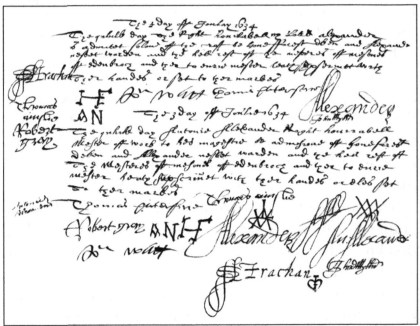

I reproduced the above document from 1634 in my *Oak Island Knights* book for the first time just as it appears in the records of Freemason Lodge #1, Edinburgh, Scotland, and as written on July 3, 1634, along with the text from this document retyped, but still in Old English as it was first penned.

It is likely that only a few people in history had ever seen this document until I reprinted it in my book. Here is the translation found in the 1873 Freemasonry book:

The 3 day off Joulay 1634. The quhilk (which) day the Right honirabell (honorable) my Lord Alexander is admitet folowe off (admitted a fellow of) the craft be (by) Hewe Forest diken (deacon), and Alexander Nesbet warden; and the hell (whole) rest off the mesteres off mesones off Edenbroch (of the masters of masons of Edinburgh); and therto eurie mester heath supscriuet (every master has subscribed) with ther handes or set to ther markes. (witnesses were) Jn. Watt, Thomas Patersone, Alexander, John Mylln.

There are similar documents for the initiations of Anthony Alexander, Al Strachan and David Ramsay.

Ramsay was closely related to Al Strachan and he not only served as a personal aid to King Charles, but also became the world's fifth non-operative, accepted Mason, on August 25, 1637. Just the year before, Lodge #1 of Edinburgh used the term Freemason for the first time, in this case as "Frie Mesones," written December 27, 1636.

Ramsay was known to be interested in the occult. In William Lilly's *Life and Times*, from 1715, an amusing account is given of an attempt made, in 1634, by David Ramsay and others, to discover hidden treasure at Westminster Abbey: "...by means of the divining rod, when the operations were interrupted by fierce blasts of wind, attributed by the terrified spectators to demons, who were, however, promptly exorcised."

Also, Sir Edward Coke, when writing to Secretary Windebanke, on May 9, 1639, stated: "If, now, David Ramsay can co-operate with his philosopher's stone, he would do a good service."

Ramsay also held a patent for extracting gold and silver from baser metals – essentially alchemy. He had a flare for the occult and was the go-between when William Alexander brought a Rosicrucian to meet the king. It is this very family who established Dalhousie University just an hour's drive from Oak Island. The cornerstone laid at the foundation of this university reveals that Lord Dalhousie, the man who founded Dalhousie University, had formerly been the Scottish Master of Masons, a position previously held by Thomas Howard, whose name appears on the 90' Stone, followed by Henry Alexander, son of Sir William Alexander.

Among those attending the laying of the cornerstone were the Grand Master of all Nova Scotia Freemasons, along with the Grand Wardens, Officers and Brethren of all Halifax Lodges. You could not tie Freemasonry any closer to Dalhousie University's beginnings than with this list of men present at the cornerstone event.

Lord Dalhousie was George Ramsay. He was related to the world's fifth Freemason, David Ramsay, who, himself, was closely related to Alexander Strachan. George's father, also named George, had been Grand Master of the Freemasons as well. His son, James Broun-Ramsay, followed in this tradition, followed again by George's nephew, Fox-Maule Ramsay, to whom the Freemasonry book was dedicated.

Ramsay has always been a very prominent name in Scottish Freemasonry. George would also be related to the current Grand Master of Scottish Freemasonry (as of this writing) William Ramsay McGhee, whose mother was Janet Ramsay. William often goes by the nickname "Ramsay."

It was in the book about Edinburgh Lodge #1 where I found the story of the treasure Al Strachan had stolen, which may have made its way to Oak Island, and also the story of the first seven Freemasons. All of them were in some way connected to the Knights Baronet or to William Alexander. One of them may actually have been William Alexander. If so, this would help verify the story told by Marsha Keith Schuchard, in her book *Restoring the Temple of Vision*.

In 1637, a man whose name is given as Alexander Alerdis was installed into Freemasonry at Edinburgh Lodge #1. His true identity has remained a mystery. He was the world's sixth Freemason, placed in between David Ramsay (of the Dalhousie University family) and Henry Alexander, son of Sir William Alexander who was given Nova Scotia, in 1621.

An essay entitled "Freemasonry on Both Sides of the Atlantic," written by three Masonic researchers (Richard William Weisberger, Wallace McLeod, and S. Brent Morris) says that, while it has been speculated that Alexander Alerdis was actually Alexander of Allardyce, they state unequivocally that: "The identity of Alerdis remains a mystery."

I may have a solution to that mystery.

Both Alexander Alerdis and David Ramsay were initiated into Freemasonry in the same year. When William Alexander Jr., joined the Freemasons, he used the name "Alexander," since he was, at the time, Lord Alexander. His brother Anthony used "Anthony Alexander," and another brother Henry used "Henry Alexander."

I think it is possible that Alerdis was simply a version or misspelling of the word "elder," and that Alexander Alerdis was actually Alexander the Elder, or Sir William Alexander Sr.

It is at least possible that William Sr. became a Freemason, as did three of his sons. And he, being the elder among all of the Freemasons of that period, was chosen as the magistrate of the so-called secret Templar / Masonic order, a position later held by David Ramsay.

There is virtually no usage of the word alderis in any search on Google. In fact, if you try to search for Alexander Alerdis, you may even be asked if you want to instead search for "Alexander Elder." At least I was.

Google, with all of its complex algorithms, and all of its billions, if not trillions, of bits of data, chooses elder to replace Alerdis.

George Black's *Surnames of Scotland*, the Bible of Scottish surname origins, gives many versions of the Allardyce name, but none of them are spelled Alerdis.

So, we have three serious Masonic historians, plus Google, plus George Black, the premier historian of Scottish surnames, all pointing away from Alerdis as meaning Allardyce.

Many other words in these early Freemason records have very odd spellings, as well. Honorable is spelled "honiraball." Whole is spelled "heall" or "hell." Ancient is spelled "antient," and often still is. Deacon is spelled "deken." Even Mason is spelled "messones," "mesone," "meson" and "maisone."

If William Alexander Sr. was, in fact, helping lead this secret Templar-Masonic order, he had to be a Freemason. And yet his initiation doesn't appear anywhere in history except, and unless, it was he who was initiated as Alexander Alderis, or Alexander the Elder.

In the book, *Memorials of the Earl of Stirling and of the House of Alexander*, by Rev. Charles Rogers, 1877, Sir William Alexander is given as Alexander the Elder twice, and his son is given as Alexander the Younger three times. The record of Alexander Alderis could actually have been Alexander the Elder to delineate him from his son, William Jr., who had earlier signed his name simply as "Alexander."

If I am correct, then four of the first seven Scottish Freemasons were from the Alexander family (of Clan Donald), who also owned Nova Scotia. And the father, William Alexander the Elder, was a leader of this form of Masonry which came to be known as Freemasonry in 1636, just one year before his 1637 initiation. Two more interesting points from the initiation of Alexander Alerdis are found in the actual record, which reads: "The twentie seven day off Desember being Sant Johnes day (1637) : The qwhilk day in presanc off the hell (whole) me'rs off mesones, and frieman off mesones off Edr."

First, we have Alexander's initiation happening on St. John's Day. St. John was the patron saint of the Knights Templar. Second, we have the differentiation being made between Master stonemasons and Freemen of Masons, or Freemasons. Records show that these early Mason lodges went out of their way to delineate between true stonemasons and non-operative Masons.

Whether he was actually Alexander Alerdis or not, there is no doubt that William Alexander had a great influence on Freemasonry since three of his sons and his partner were among the first seven known Freemasons.

After the loss of the Scots settlement at Port Royal, Nova Scotia, in 1632, the Alexanders entered Masonry in 1634, along with David Ramsay in 1637, but as honorary members, not stonemasons.

Author Marsha Keith Schuchard writes that Charles I was actually nicknamed "the Mason King," for his support of the organization. In fact, Freemason sources indicate that King Charles took over as Scottish Master of Masons from 1625 through 1630 at which time he turned the role over to Henry Danvers, Earl of Derby, who then relinquished it to Thomas Howard, Earl of Arundel, who passed it on to Henry Alexander in 1639.

Schuchard also states that David Ramsay became the magistrate of this new Templar inspired organization, later called the Freemasons, upon the death of Sir William Alexander in 1640.

In 1641, according to Alexander family history, Henry's brother, John Alexander, returned to what is now the New Ross area of Nova Scotia until 1654.

In a few of my books I've taken the time to summarize the story in order that it can be best understood. That may be as important with this book as with any of my others simply because the material is new and a little bit complex.

To begin with, we know humankind has engaged in two specific practices pertinent to this story.

First, we have the use of symbols to represent words and ideas. The old saying is that "a picture is worth a thousand words." The same is true for a symbol and I have shown examples of this practice from ancient cave drawings to modern-day smart phone emojis, with dozens more in between. Freemasonry itself is filled with symbology.

It may have been an incorrect first step for the finders of the 90' Stone to assume the translation would consist of a letter-for-letter substitution rather than look at the symbology behind the message. Certainly, the MQS (or Mary, Queen of Scots) code matches every symbol on the stone except for one – the three dot triangle being a known Freemason code for "Scottish Master of Masons" and used thousands of times in Freemason literature.

This symbol could be the first proven link of Freemasonry's involvement in the Money Pit on Oak Island, and that is significant in itself.

Second, humans have used written curses throughout recorded history, many of which were carved on a stone and buried underground, similar to the Money Pit 90' Stone. Some curse stones could more appropriately be referred to as prayer stones, calling on "holy beings."

The Oak Island curse had to originate somewhere. Where could that be?

I have provided not only a potential treasure buried in the Money Pit (the treasure stolen by Al Strachan in 1622) but also a treasure that came with its own curse, the curse from the Abbey of Deer. This curse is proven to have come true in the demise of Earl Marischal George Keith, the man Strachan robbed. If the money changed hands to Al Strachan, and then to Oak Island, why couldn't the curse follow it?

We know that some of these "curse tablet" creators called on higher powers to assist them in their ventures or to protect their treasures. The first line of the 90' Stone code follows this pattern in imploring "O, God send angels," when the MQS codex is used to translate it. We also know that the names of Thomas Howard, a proven Scottish Master of Masons, and his son Henry, also appear on the 90' Stone. This family was intimately involved with Mary, Queen of Scots, and with her four kingly descendants whose actions had such a lasting impact on Nova Scotia.

In addition, Thomas Howard was connected to early settlements in New England and Nova Scotia, and to Shakespeare and Sir Francis Bacon. Bacon died at Howard's home, and Howard is thought to have met with Shakespeare many times. We also know that Howard was associated with Sir William Alexander both in the beginning of Freemasonry and through Alexander's 1624 map of Nova Scotia. Both men also served on the Council or Commission for Fishing.

I have proposed that this Fishing Council was a secret spy organization meant to keep track of the happenings in Nova Scotia through the use of innocent looking fishing fleets. Well, guess what. This practice still continues. China and Vietnam are, even today, heavily involved in reconnaissance of each other through fishing vessels. And fishing vessels have always had a sort of hands-off protection applied to them in Maritime law.

Thomas Howard and William Alexander served on this Fishing Council along with ten additional men, all having links either to the Knights Baronet of Nova Scotia, to Shakespeare and Sir Francis Bacon, to the history of Mary, Queen of Scots, or to Freemasonry.

We also know that Thomas Howard was the Scottish Master of Masons when William Alexander's sons, William Jr. and Anthony, along with his partner, Al Strachan, were initiated as the world's first-known non-operative Masons, or what we would today all a Freemason.

We can also easily see that both the years 1625 and 1632 were significant in this story.

In 1625, Al Strachan was given a full pardon for his crime of robbing George Keith, and was made a partner with Sir William Alexander in his Nova Scotia venture. Also, in this year, the Knights Baronet of Nova Scotia were founded and each knight paid the equivalent of $500,000 in current U.S. dollars. This settlement of Nova Scotia was not a small potatoes operation. Finally, in 1625, King Charles I became the Scottish Master of Masons adding the ultimate credibility to these lodges.

Turning to the year 1632, we have Thomas Howard making plans to leave on a trip of undetermined length and purpose, beginning in January. Also in 1632, Henry Howard is accepted on the Council of New England.

By March 29, 1632, the Scots who were settled at Port Royal, Nova Scotia, were asked to leave due to a treaty with France over ownership of Nova Scotia that favored the French over the Scots Knights Baronet.

I have proposed for several years now that the Money Pit was constructed in April, May and June of 1632 (or around that basic time period). Gilbert Hedden, former owner and searcher of Oak Island, wrote to Franklin Roosevelt that he thought the Money Pit could have been built as early as 1635. He wrote to another person, in 1967, that he felt that it was built around 1630 and could have been accomplished by a small crew in about three to four months. This last point has been agreed to recently by two additional engineers, Les MacPhie and Graham Harris, who studied the Money Pit and Oak Island very closely and wrote a popular book about it.

Many items have been carbon dated, or otherwise dated, that fit my target date of 1632, from a Scottish ox shoe (as old as 1610) to axe cut wood found deep in the Money Pit area (as old as 1626), to many items found in other places around the island. Another example is a carpenter's square dating to as old as 1632, found near the stone road in the Oak Island swamp.

Following the return of Alexander's settlers, in June of 1632, a Fishing Council was set up in July of the same year and was led by men significant to my story.

Also, at the very end of the year, on December 25, 1632, the *Grand Lodge Manuscript* of Freemasonry was written attempting to extoll virtues in Masons, especially loyalty to God and King, and also in the living of a good life so as not to bring shame on the craft of Masonry.

It wasn't until Sir William Alexander and his friend David Ramsay entered the picture that Freemasonry, as we now know it, began to take shape with the addition of esoteric and ceremonial elements.

Sir William Alexander founded Nova Scotia in 1621. Later, the family of David Ramsay founded Dalhousie University about an hour's drive from Oak Island. The University has been involved with the island in many ways in the past, with the Oak Island Association meeting there, with Freemasons meeting there, with one of its professors being involved in translating the 90' Stone, and another in writing a fiction version of the Oak Island story. There are even rumors of a stash of Oak Island artifacts stored at the university.

David Ramsay was not only the fifth known non-operative Mason ever initiated, but he was also a practitioner of the occult, including using a dowsing rod and his ownership of a philosopher's stone, in addition to being a fan of the Rosicrucian/cabalistic movement.

The founder of the university, George Ramsay, Lord Dalhousie, had just retired as Scottish Master of Masons, a position also held by his father, his son, his nephew, and the current leader of Freemasonry in Scotland, William Ramsay McGhee, whose mother was Janet Ramsay. William goes by the nickname "Ramsay."

As for the Howard family, Thomas Howard's own grandfather was found with Mary, Queen of Scots' codex hidden under his floor tile and he was executed for treason. I believe it is possible that a codex known by the descendants of Mary, Queen of Scots, and by the family of Thomas Howard, could easily have been used to leave a prayer tablet behind on Oak Island to protect the Money Pit treasure and to ask God for support for Thomas Howard, the historically known Scottish Master of Masons and friend of William Alexander, Shakespeare and Sir Francis Bacon.

There are key connections not only of the Knights Templar to Freemasonry, but also of Freemasonry to Nova Scotia, both of which were aided by the Knights Baronet of Nova Scotia, and by Sir William Alexander, David Ramsay and Thomas Howard, with help from Charles I and Sir Francis Bacon. These events are backed by historical evidence, not something I've invented.

As with most things in life, I think the establishment of Freemasonry was overdetermined – in other words several events and influences conspired to create the Freemasons. Among these were:

- A desire to protect significant knowledge kept alive in the geometry / skills used by the building trades;
- A desire to regain lost knowledge;
- A desire to discover new knowledge using the study of the Natural World;
- A desire to develop esoteric ways of retaining this knowledge through memory techniques, symbols and ceremonies;

- A desire on the part of William Alexander, Thomas Howard and others to have control over the powerful stonemasons who generated wealth by applying secretive building techniques, especially after the demise of the Knights Baronet and the loss of the fur, fishing, minerals and lumber wealth of Nova Scotia;
- A desire to celebrate and incorporate the traditions of groups like the Knights Templar and Rosicrucians into a new group – the Freemasons;
- A practical effort on the part of William Alexander to have his son Anthony invested in the position of Master of (Public) Works, overseeing stonemason lodges at the objection of William Sinclair of Rosslyn Chapel, a longtime patron of the stonemasons.

Based on the dates of these early records, Sir Francis Bacon could not have been a Freemason, although he does seem to have helped create a pattern for it.

I think the reasons for so much secrecy were also over determined. Likely, one was to protect wealth-generating techniques practiced in stonemasonry. Another was to avoid public censure or worse – political or religious persecution for ideas that went against the norm of the day. Another may have been to keep newly discovered knowledge quiet until the bearers of it could financially benefit from it. In addition, there was the plagiarism factor, which Bacon seemed quite worried about. There are also many historically recorded instances of backstabbing, duplicity and abandonment, or even beheading of once valued associates, during the 1600s, which the Freemasons could help prevent.

King Charles himself was a practitioner of some of these undesireable traits. In the end, he was the victim of his own devices when he became the one and only "British" monarch ever to be beheaded. (Mary, Queen of Scots, was Scottish not British).

The roots of Freemasonry were growing in Scotland during this time period of the reign of Charles I, the writings of Bacon, a growing interest in Jewish cabalism, and the exploration and settlement of the New World.

This resulted in William Alexander's three sons, his business partner Al Strachan, and his Rosicrucian friend David Ramsay, becoming five out of the first seven recorded Freemasons, and his son, Henry, becoming the Scottish Master of Freemasonry after Thomas Howard.

As I've pointed out, another early Freemason may have been William Alexander himself, and the final one was a Stewart cousin of King Charles, connected to the Knights Baronet and likely installed as a Freemason in order to report back to King Charles about the activities this new organization was involved in.

Other families like the MacDonalds and Macleans played an important role in the Knights Baronet of Nova Scotia, in Freemasonry, and in the very establishment of British settlements in Nova Scotia (and throughout Canada) as well as in the specific history of Oak Island.

This review is somewhat the nutshell version of my theory and of the beginning of Freemasonry, and gives a pretty good indication of how it all fits together to form a story about the 90' Stone that is extremely coincidental, if not true. And, there's more to come!

Chapter Nine
BEHIND DOOR NUMBER ONE

When deciding on what I wanted the cover of this book to look like, I knew I wanted an old door which led into a mystical building, a temple of sorts. I also liked the lock on this particular door as it seemed it could possibly be broken to give access to what was inside.

The one thing about this door was that it was the entrance to an old Jewish temple, and I thought to myself, "I hope no one gets upset that I am stealing a Jewish work of craftsmanship to talk about Scotsmen."

This thought gave me pause several times over the next few months as I would open up my book files to begin writing about my latest research. But still, the door epitomized the look and feel I wanted for this book, and so I went with it. Little did I know that, once again, the Oak Island muses were dangling a clue in front of my nose all that time.

Whether we love our own nose or hate it, there's no getting away from the fact that the nose is the most protruding part of the face and one of our most distinguishable features. From tribal ornaments and modern-day piercing to Hollywood nose jobs – it's no wonder that humans throughout history have made such an effort to help this body part look good.

But the history of nose beauty ideals has been changeable and at times dark. For example, in early Europe the prominent "Roman Nose" signified beauty and nobility. The Nazis on the other hand despised it and saw it as a characteristic strictly of Jewish people.

This type of distinguishable nose is owned by millions of people all over the world and yet is often called the "Roman Nose" or the "Jewish Nose." A more appropriate description might be the "Mediterranean Nose."

When I first saw the most common image of Sir William Alexander, I was struck by the size of his nose. He certainly didn't look "Scottish," and no one in my Scottish family (a family related to Alexander in the distant past) had a nose approaching his in size. In the end, I blew this off thinking the poor guy was just an aberration in the family line. Every once in awhile I'd see a painting of another nobleman from that time with a somewhat similar large nose, and often a darker complexion, but again I didn't give it much thought.

In researching Freemasonry, I finally got my hands on a copy of Shuchard's 800-page masterpiece, *Restoring the Temple of Vision*, on the origins of secret societies particularly in Scotland and England, which often mentioned Jewish cabalism as a beginning point.

In it, the author speaks of the influence of cabalistic rituals in the formation of belief systems for the Rosicrucians and the Freemasons. In other literature, this was sometimes attributed to the years the Knights Templar spent in the Holy Land fighting in the Crusades or protecting pilgrims at the Holy City of Jerusalem.

They were also rumored to have found the Jewish Menorah and/or the Ark of the Covenant, two items often associated with Oak Island lore. In addition, we have the Tree of Life that is sometimes compared to Nolan's Cross on Oak Island, even though they are not even remotely similar beyond having a long shaft going up the middle. The Tree of Life has many more "arms" to it and none are in a position resembling any cross, especially Nolan's Cross.

Still, the idea of Jewish artifacts or symbols on Oak Island has been a hard one to squelch.

Giovanni Francesco Barbieri (b.1591–d.1666), better known as Guercino, was an Italian Baroque painter who was active in Rome. His painting *Et in Arcadia ego,* from around 1618–1622, contains the first known usage anywhere of this Latin motto (later taken up by another painter named Poussin). This phrase signifies that death lurks even in the most idyllic settings.

Poussin's painting of the same name has also been associated with Oak Island in the minds of a few theorists, since an early name for Nova Scotia was Acadia, supposedly taken from Arcadia.

Et in Arcadia ego translates as "I too in Arcadia" or, in other words, "I (death) am also present in Arcadia" (which was the Greek ideal of Paradise). It is a fact that William Alexander was in Rome in the exact same year as Poussin (1624) meeting with Poussin's benefactor on a separate matter of getting a dispensation for the Protestant English King Charles I to marry the Catholic Princess Henrietta Maria, sister to the French king.

What's interesting is that Guercino also painted another masterpiece entitled *Abraham Casting Out Hagar and Ishmael*, shown below.

Abraham is considered the progenitor of the Jewish race and yet, in Guercino's painting, Abraham's nose, though looking a lot like an older man's nose, is definitely not a stereotypical Mediterranean nose.

Obviously, Guercino did not have Abraham available to pose for him, but he did live and work in Rome where Mediterranean noses were likely found all around him everyday. Since this painter was known for his realism, it would seem that the idea of a more prominent nose for Jewish people was not a "thing" back then.

Whether it came about through anti-Semitism or just a few prominent examples of this facial feature in people, paintings or writings is hard to determine. But the plain fact is that larger noses are found all over the world, from the Mayans to Scotland - yes, I said Scotland.

Below is the most common image to be found of William Alexander, the one that gave me pause due to his prominent nose.

This image appeared in a collection of Alexander's works called *Recreation of the Muses* from 1637. Very few copies of this book included this portrait of William Alexander, engraved by William Marshall, so "first state" or original press run copies of this print are very scarce. Due to this scarcity, William Richardson produced a reasonable copy in 1795.

Until recently, this overall image reproduced in several versions, was the only image of William Alexander – that is until I found the location of a 1634 painting of King Charles I handing a document to Alexander. I used this painting on the front cover of my last book *Oak Island And New Ross*. In that image William Alexander also has a prominent nose as does King Charles. In fact, Mary, Queen of Scots (see page 72), and her four Stewart descendants, who each became King of Great Britain, all had prominent noses.

In the book *When Scotland Was Jewish*, by Elizabeth Caldwell Hirschman and Donald N. Yates (2007), the authors used "DNA Evidence, Archeology, Analysis of Migrations, and Public and Family Records" to show possible Semitic roots for some Scottish clans.

Two of the clans mentioned as possibly having Jewish roots are the Alexanders and the Stewarts. According to the book *History of the Lodge of Edinburgh #1*, by David Lyon (1873), three if not four of the first seven recorded non-operative Masons (or what we would now call Freemasons) were from the Alexander family and another was from the Stewart family. Yet another, David Ramsay, was enamored with esoteric beliefs.

ABOVE: Four descendants of Mary, Queen of Scots, all sporting reasonably prominent noses. They are: 1) James I, first King of what he called "Great Britain" – granted Nova Scotia to William Alexander; 2) Charles I – knighted all Knights Baronet of Nova Scotia until 1649; 3) Charles II – knighted Thomas Temple as the last Knight Baronet to receive land in Nova Scotia; and 4) James II – knighted Sir William Phips.

In the 1857 book *Jewish Literature from the Eighth to the Eighteenth Century,* by Moritz Steinschneider, the author shows how dozens and dozens of Jewish writings from the 8th through the 16th centuries were full of thoughts on astronomy, astrology, geomancy, second sight (which became so popular in Scotland that it prompted the first modern scientific study of this phenomenon), palm reading, philosopher's stones and other esoteric beliefs. These Jewish writings also captured a great amount of history of ancient Greece, Egypt and Rome. Some of the above subjects were part of Jewish cabalism, which itself has been credited with sparking similar interests in secret societies like the Rosicrucians and Freemasons.

I haven't completely read the previously mentioned book, *When Scotland Was Jewish,* yet but what I've seen shows that some stretches of the imagination were used to prove some points, while other ideas present enough data to warrant close study. The book certainly draws on many aspects of early Scottish life to prove the authors' main point that at least some Scottish clans might have had Jewish blood in their veins, which could be true since Scotland has been a "melting pot" for a long time.

One of the principal tools the authors use is to present contemporary images of many noblemen in Scotland, some that coincidentally have direct connections with my theory. When I read this, I realized that perhaps my curiosity about Sir William Alexander's facial features was not that far out of line. He and many of the people that he was nearest to tended to feature a prominent Mediterranean nose, as shown in the following images.

We begin with William Alexander's tutor and major Scottish historian, George Buchanan, who was not only painted with his beard and prominent nose but also with a head covering similar to the men's skullcap known in Judaism as a kippah, or yamaka. Buchanan was also tutor for Mary, Queen of Scots.

Next up, we have Alexander's very first student and also his traveling companion in Europe, Archibald Campbell. In Gaelic, Archibald is typically written as *Gylascop* (Note how this is very similar to Glooscap, the Mi'kmaq hero).

Here we can once again take note of the prominent nose and the similar yamaka type head covering.

The family of Sir Robert Gordon held the position of the "premier" or first Knight Baronet of Nova Scotia until 1908 when that line died out and the second-positioned knighthood moved into the premier position – that of my distant kinsman Sir Ian MacDonald MacUisdean.

Gordon, shown here, also sports a prominent nose.

The surname of Gordon is one of the more common Jewish surnames.

Sir Robert Gordon owned 16,000 acres of land near the east end of Port Mouton, Nova Scotia, which is less than 60 miles from Oak Island.

Gordon carried out military/intelligence missions for Kings James I and Charles I, and was a liaison between Charles I and his bride to be, Henrietta Maria, until William Alexander could affect the special dispensation from the pope for their marriage.

Below is John Knox, the fiery Scottish Presbyterian preacher who led the Reformation in Scotland. Knox opposed Mary, Queen of Scots, and it was his religious movement that led directly to the demise of William Alexander and to the beheading of Charles I. Again, note the prominent Mediterranean nose.

Knox was raised Roman Catholic but promoted the Presbyterian religion. Meanwhile, the surname Knox is a very common Eastern European Jewish name.

IOANNES CNOXVS, SCOTVS.

What could account for all these grim, large-nosed Scottish noblemen (along with many other possible examples), some wearing long Biblical quality beards, and some wearing a head piece similar to a Hebrew yamaka?

There are a few possible answers:

• First, perhaps some if not all of these men did have Jewish or at least Mediterranean blood in them;

• Second, perhaps prominent noses were actually a Scottish trait that has to some degree subsided and has never actually been studied in this detail before;

• Third, perhaps these noses were exaggerated by the artist, since a prominent nose had long denoted a strong leader, a theory that traces all the way back to Roman and Greek men like Julius Caesar and Pythagoras.

The most logical theory is that these paintings represent, fairly closely, what these men actually looked like. So the unique facial features, if not from a Mediterranean background, have to be explained somehow. One thing is certain, Jewish cabalism played a role in the foundation of secret societies like the Rosicrucians and Freemasons based on an abundance of evidence in Shuchard's book and in many other books.

We've talked a lot about symbols but perhaps the greatest one meant to replace a word or idea is the Jewish symbol for the name of God, typically known as a Tetragrammaton. This Jewish symbol, shown below, was found emblazoned on the title page of a 1623 Christian Book of Psalms, in Glasgow, Scotland.

The yamaka styled hats can also be explained as being symbolic. While Jews often wear a yamaka or kippah, Catholic priests, bishops and cardinals often wear a very similar looking headgear known as a zucchetto, also worn by some Anglican ministers.

In turn, scholars wore a variety of skullcaps, including some that resembled a yamaka or zucchetto. Others wore silk wraps as hats. There was another reason for wearing these caps beyond simply keeping the head warm – status.

Just as businessmen wear a tie or doctors wear a stethoscope around their neck, various orders of knighthood wore their own style of head gear (for example the Knights Templar). Scholars wore a simple skullcap to denote seriousness in their studies and also to highlight their position as a scholar in the minds of the public. The yamaka styled caps worn by the men in the previous photos should not necessarily be taken to mean they were definitely of the Jewish religion or race, but may have been simply denoting their scholastic endeavors.

There is one thing curious about being Jewish – the name can mean your religion or it can mean your race, unlike a Catholic or Protestant who could be of nearly any ethnicity.

Referring to someone as Jewish doesn't necessarily denote their race, and vice versa. A Jew could convert to the Catholic or Protestant religion and still be Jewish in race. A Catholic or Protestant could convert to Judaism but still be of a race that contains no Jewish blood.

During the 17th century, some men in Scotland, prominent nose or not, may have been fascinated with Jewish cabalism as the one-God religion predating Christianity. Those inclined to mysticism or esoteric ways may have been fascinated by it for other reasons.

We also have to consider the Declaration of Arbroath, from 1320, constituting Robert the Bruce's response to his excommunication for disobeying the pope's demand in 1317, for a truce in the First War of Scottish Independence. The letter asserted the antiquity of the independence of the Kingdom of Scotland. Two phrases from this document are very interesting:

•*We know from the deeds of the ancients and we read from books -- because among the other great nations of course, our nation of Scots has been described in many publications -- that crossing from Greater Scythia, via the Tyrhennian Sea and the Pillars of Hercules, and living in Spain among the fiercest tribes for many years, it could be conquered by no one anywhere, no matter how barbarous the tribes. Afterwards, coming from there, one thousand two hundred years from the Israelite people's crossing of the Red Sea, to its home in the west, which it now holds.;*

•*From these countless evils, with His help who afterwards soothes and heals wounds, we are freed by our tireless leader, king, and master, Lord Robert, who like another Maccabaeus or Joshua, underwent toil and tiredness, hunger and danger with a light spirit in order to free the people and his inheritance from the hands of his enemies.*

In addition, we have the Stone of Destiny. The basic tale is that the stone was the pillow Jacob laid his head on when he fell asleep and dreamed of the Biblical Jacob's Ladder, which, in some interpretations, signified the exiles which the Jewish people would suffer before the coming of the Jewish messiah.

The story is that the Stone of Destiny was brought to Ireland by Scota, a Pharoah's daughter, who also gave her name to Scotland, when the stone and her followers, known as the Scotti, moved there. Scotti-land eventually became Scotland, as the story goes. There is currently a Stone of Destiny on display in Edinburgh Castle, which may or may not be the historical one (see my first book *Oak Island Missing Links*).

Not to be outdone, the bagpipes have a Middle Eastern origin as well and some modern pipes are still made there. And let's not forget Solomon's Temple and the Knights Templar connection. Along with all of the above, it is also true that knights from Scotland were engaged in fighting to protect the Jewish Holy Land.

The book *When Scotland was Jewish* mentions some symbology in Scotland (in coats of arms and building decorations) that includes the Islamic crescent and stars (as does William Alexander's personal coat of arms), and that the Star of David appeared on Scottish coins from the 13th century. Also mentioned is the fact that the Campbells of Argyll located their castle at a place called Succoth, which is not only the name of a major Jewish holiday, but also the place name of a few locations in the Middle East.

Finally, we have DNA research and its sister science of protein analysis of human blood samples. Both point to the fact that throughout most of the European continent, the majority of genetic diversity shows migration from the southeast towards the northwest, or in other words from the Middle East towards Scotland and Ireland, just as Scottish legends imply.

We seem to have science, societal legends and various known examples described in this chapter joining forces to present a very possible Middle Eastern origin of the Scottish race. Without any doubt, there was a fascination in Scotland with the Middle East, with Jewish cabalism, with "protecting" the Holy Land through the Crusades, and with Middle Eastern symbolism.

The book *When Scotland Was Jewish* also points out that Prince Michael Stewart, the supposed heir or "pretender" to the Stewart dynasty of Scotland, also happens to be the Honorary President of the Association of Jewish Students of Glasgow University.

In addition, the subtitle for Shuchard's book, *The Restoring of the Temple of Vision,* is: *Cabalistic Freemasonry and Stuart (Stewart) Culture.*

I am not 100% sold on either book but they both hold some information that might help explain the formation of both the Rosicrucians and the Freemasons based on cabalistic beliefs, especially within Scotland among the friends and family of Sir William Alexander. Of note, Alexander wrote in his 1617 *Doomes-Day* book: "America to Europe may succeed/God may of stones raise up to Abraham's seed."

Chapter Ten
BACON WITH THAT?

In nearly every area of my research and theory, Sir Francis Bacon is involved. He was on the Privy Council with Sir William Alexander, and both were creative authors. He was involved in the Plymouth Colony reorganization, and he knew Thomas Howard, Earl of Arundel, well, and died at his home.

Sir Francis Bacon seemed aware that his scientific writings were only the beginning of a much larger movement in 17th century Great Britain to regain "secret" knowledge of the past, and to gain new knowledge by observing nature and by carrying out a wide variety of experiments in many disparate areas.

Beyond just normal human curiosity, this pursuit of knowledge may have been driven by a few factors.

One was simply that there was plenty of evidence of lost knowledge. For instance, the Romans were able to pour concrete and have it harden underwater. The secret of this method was not rediscovered until the mid 1700s when a lighthouse using similar components for its underwater concrete was built near Plymouth, England. Scientists are still today exploring this Roman technique and making new discoveries as to why it was so successful.

There were other mysteries to understand, some we still struggle with today, such as how large stones weighing several tons were raised into the air at places like Stonehenge and the Pyramids of Giza, and at so many other ancient sites around the world.

Today it would take mammoth heavy equipment to complete the same task. I've seen the Great Wall of China, the Pyramids, Machu Picchu, Chichen Itza and other similar sites, in person and first-hand, and "they ain't chopped liver," as they say.

Since the days of Solomon's Temple, the secrets of the building trade remained just that. One obvious reason was that there was money to be made in having proprietary information on how to construct large edifices like cathedrals, castles, bridges and other immense buildings that would stand the test of time.

Another driving force was that the British Isles were becoming barren of minerals, timber and arable land. As William Alexander put it, the inhabitants were obliged to rely mostly on fishing for their food and occupation, or to engage in piracy and war with other countries, like France and Spain, in order to gain new wealth.

The New World offered great promise in providing silver, gold and other important metals through mining, plus lumber, furs and other natural resources long since depleted at home.

Bacon knew that the only way to get the ball moving on pursuing the effort to regain lost knowledge, discover new knowledge and to promote immigration to the New World, was to write about it.

He stated in one of his works, "This writing seemeth to me not much better than the noise and sound musicians make while they are tuning their instruments; which is nothing pleasant to hear, but yet is a cause why the music is sweeter afterwards: so I have been content to tune the instruments of the Muses, that they may play who have better hands."

In his book *The New Atlantis*, Bacon writes of a "red cross" governor who tells of secret knowledge used to build a "magnificent temple" on a hill, to which men ascend by "several degrees." In his mythical utopia, which he named Bensalem, Bacon tells of the House of Salomon and suggests a link between the "Art of Memory" and the natural sciences.

The Art of Memory, loosely defined, includes using symbols such as the Mason's Mark, or the Mark of Merchant Adventurers (early trademarks), plus other devices like memorable poems that would help stir the memory, along with visualization and other techniques.

Many of these same techniques are used today in marketing efforts and devices found in the study of neuro-linguistic programming, and also in meditation techniques. Think company logos and ad jingles.

Among Bensalem's "Merchants of Light" there were three who collected "the experiments of all mechanical arts, liberal sciences, and practices which are not brought into arts." These three men are called "Mystery-men," while there are also "novices and apprentices" who take an oath of secrecy "for the concealing of those (inventions and experiments) which we think fit to keep secret."

Bacon's writings seem to be a pattern for Freemasonry. He is sometimes said to be a Freemason, but history shows us that he died in 1626, eight years before the first non-operative Masons were installed – these being the sons of his fellow Privy Council member, poet and adventurer in the New World, Sir William Alexander.

While I am still focused on a treasure being buried on Oak Island by followers of the Knights Baronet of Nova Scotia, I have, from the very beginning, put forth the idea that Francis Bacon passed some of his scientific papers on to William Alexander to be taken to the New World for posterity and for safekeeping. I think this is more likely than Shakespeare's papers, although there are a lot of believers in the theory that Shakespeare's plays and poetry lie at the bottom of the Money Pit.

The logic is that Bacon and others, including Sir William Alexander, were the actual authors of most of Shakespeare's work and did not want to risk prison or worse for the anti-royalty nature of some of them.

Still, Bacon was so pragmatic, especially about science, that I feel he'd more likely want his scientific papers protected and his theories used in the New World.

There is virtually no way that Sir Francis Bacon was not keenly aware of William Alexander's Nova Scotia plan. It was backed by the king that they both served, and it involved many Scottish clan chieftains and well-known, powerful Englishmen. Each of these men served in high-level governmental positions and on the Privy Council of the king together. So it is likely that they knew each other very well.

Bacon and Alexander were both writers of poems, plays and books, and both dreamed of a united Great Britain. They also dreamed of a utopia to be created in North America. Bacon could have easily imposed on his friend to take some of his writings to the New World for posterity. It is known that Bacon was concerned with plagiarism and censorship, and it is reported that he had considered burying his manuscripts, and had discussed using mercury as a preservative. Mercury, or mercury flasks, were said to be found in or around the Money Pit on Oak Island.

Bacon also wrote of a technique that was used to preserve documents by placing them in a canvas bag and sealing them with candle wax. This was exactly how the title deeds to George Keith's castles were protected, and this type of bag is mentioned in the list of treasure stolen by Al Strachan.

Parchment was pulled up from the Money Pit with the India ink not smeared, even though the pit had been flooded for decades. The only way this could have happened is if the parchment was kept in a waterproof container that was pierced by the drill bit that brought the parchment to the surface.

When the current Oak Island team recently found parchment and bookbinding it was stained purple, no doubt from the India ink dissolving in the water.

So the parchment could have been Bacon's writings or it could have been Keith's title-deeds, or it could have been something unknown to us, but that somehow made its way a hundred feet or more underground.

It's certainly plausible that William Alexander's men took part of Strachan's stolen treasure to Nova Scotia to help finance the new colony, and that they were also asked to take some of Bacon's scientific papers to be used to establish this New World utopia.

How Thomas Howard was connected to this effort is yet to be discovered, but the one thing I know about Oak Island research is that significant information seems to come out of nowhere, just about the time you think you've seen (or read) it all.

Without any doubt, Bacon knew Thomas Howard and died in his house. Bacon knew William Alexander and, like him, had also invested in the New World. In fact, his Newfoundland grant extended to Cape Breton, Nova Scotia, nearly overlapping Alexander's grant.

Bacon had concerns about his writings, even exploring ways to protect them that included burying them wrapped in waxed canvas with a bit of mercury added to ward off insects that might ruin the buried papers.

I don't, for a minute, doubt that it is possible some of Sir Francis Bacon's writings made it into the Money Pit.

Research into the relationships of Sir Francis Bacon, Sir William Alexander and Thomas Howard, Earl of Arundel, needs to continue in order to help solve the "why" of the Oak Island mystery.

And, of course, I will hopefully be very near the forefront in this research, especially with the support that has been shown to me by the Oak Island team for my theory and my yearly presentations (every year since 2017). What a great trip it has been!

Epilogue

"Oak Island is not so much a mystery to be solved as it is a chance to experience the unapologetic fascination of youth once again." – These words of mine appear on the wall of the Oak Island Interpretive Centre.

Writing a book is a daunting task and I've now written eight Oak Island volumes. It has become habit-forming due to the subject matter being so fascinating.

Because of these books I've also been invited many times to Oak Island, one of the most curious places on earth. Due to Covid restrictions, the year 2021 presented its own special challenges in getting to the island.

Crossing the border at Buffalo, New York, took me about two hours, plus a fist full of paperwork prepared by Prometheus Entertainment attesting to my importance to Oak Island research. They even wrote a letter of recommendation to the Canadian Border Service stating: "As one of the key researchers with Oak Island Tours, Inc., James A. McQuiston's on-screen appearances are critical to the production and unique theories that only he can provide." In addition, at the end of the 2020-21 season Rick Lagina made the on-air statement: "When you ask the who, what, when, where, why and how, I think James, above all the others, really deals with that… I can tell you what, James is not giving up."

Whether you, the reader, accept my theories, in part or in whole, two things you can be sure of are that my books are well-researched, and that the Oak Island team supports that research completely.

Hundreds of hours have been spent in my studio working on this mystery, and dozens more have been spent in historical institutions and on Oak Island.

War Room meetings, face-to-face meetings, emails and even phone calls have allowed me to keep the Oak Island team up-to-date on my newest finds, and it has been very exciting to share my research with them.

Despite all the great history, it has always been important to "put an X on the ground" and this is what I have figuratively tried to do with this book. Since we know the 90' Stone is said to have been at the bottom of the Money Pit on Oak Island, determining why it was put there was my goal, in hopes that this could answer additional questions about what might be, or might have been, buried there.

During my 2021 visit, Rick and the team showed me activities and artifacts that I was required to keep mum about (just as in earlier years). Watching these discoveries being made public during the 2021-22 season of *The Curse of Oak Island* has been a true joy.

But even what is shown on the weekly series, or what is written in my books, can never present all that is happening on the island. It is a giant task to chase so many leads, apply for permits, schedule equipment, fight Mother Nature, study the past, and project future moves. It is only through the determination of Rick and the Oak Island team that this is happening and maybe someday, together or individually, we'll finally crack the nut which is Oak Island. No one knows what the future holds, but I'll continue to be fascinated until the end.

ACKNOWLEDGEMENTS

As I have done in all of my Oak Island books, I would like to thank my wife, Elizabeth, who puts up with my endless hours of research and writing, and then struggles through it all to find my mistakes, or to make suggestions for improvements to my books.

Her efforts are mirrored by my cousin Pat who has taught writing in a scholastic environment and has been a great fan of my work as well.

Between these two great women I get away with virtually no misplaced punctuations, run-on sentences, misspelled words or unclear ideas. They've made my books better and I truly appreciate this.

Next, of course, my thanks go out to Rick Lagina who has believed in me like no one else, and to the entire Oak Island and Prometheus teams who have embraced my work and welcomed me to the island many times.

For this particular book I was incredibly aided by the National Archives of the UK, who identified, sorted and scanned the pertinent codex sheets of Mary, Queen of Scots, to create my one-of-a-kind digital collection of 104 sheets containing many examples of her secret code.

I'd also like to thank all those researchers and authors who have come before me, who have recorded events, uncovered information, pieced together time lines, and passed vital information directly on to me, so that I could present a theory based on historical documents, motives, a little science and known (though sometimes muddled) history. Thank you all for making this book possible.

MORE BOOKS BY THIS AUTHOR
(Books available on amazon.com)

Oak Island And New Ross – This is one of the most favorite books I have written. In it, I explore the close connection between Oak Island and a small town located about 17 miles above it along Gold River. I show how an ancient foundation at New Ross may be connected in several ways to my overall Oak Island theory and provide some real surprises, including a significant 1634 painting, an outstanding GPS discovery, and much, much more.

Oak Island And The Mayflower – In this book I show the close connection between those who arrived on the ship *Mayflower*, or within the next few years, and the early settlers and searchers of Oak Island, especially in the case of Franklin Delano Roosevelt, but many others as well.

Oak Island The Novel – This book is my attempt to tell the bigger story behind my Oak Island theory, while couching it in the form of an historical fiction novel, full of great love affairs, swashbuckling action, and a stolen treasure. All of the characters are real historic figures and all of the major events are real.

Oak Island Endgame – My first three non-fiction Oak Island books focused on the events leading up to the burial of treasure on Oak Island. With this book, I began looking at the people who came to Oak Island, as soon as it was safe for them, as landowners or searchers for treasure. This eventually led to my book *Oak Island And The Mayflower*.

Oak Island Knights – I reveal a massive treasure stolen in Scotland that appears to have been at least partially intended to finance Nova Scotia and that, due to unexpected circumstances, may have ended up buried on Oak Island. I also explore a 1671 knighthood medallion that was found at New Ross about twenty miles from Oak Island.

Oak Island 1632 – My second book on Oak Island pinpoints a specific year for the beginning of the Oak Island mystery. In it is revealed, for the first time ever, that the world's first recorded non-operative Masons all had connections to the Scots adventure in Nova Scotia, dating from 1621 to 1656. I tell how these Scots were forced to leave in bad weather, which caused them to take shelter on Oak Island.

Oak Island Missing Links – My first Oak Island book takes a new look at stories surrounding Oak Island, Nova Scotia, with some plausible interpretations of the legends of Glooscap, Henry Sinclair and the Knights Templar.

Captain Jack: Father of the Yukon – The story of the first 25 years before the Klondike Gold Rush, and the man who led the way, earning in his own lifetime the monikers of Father of the Yukon, Father of Alaska, and Yukon Jack.

Ebenezer Denny: First Mayor of Pittsburgh – The story of a man who had already led a full life as a privateer and a Revolutionary War hero before becoming the first mayor of this important frontier town.

Patrick's Run – An historical fiction account of Patrick Fitzpatrick, a hero of the War of 1812, wrongfully executed, leading to the banning of the death penalty in Michigan.

REFERENCE MATERIAL

I've used many resources over the years to understand Scottish and Oak Island history. A few worth mentioning, in regard to this particular book, are listed here in chronological order, by year of publication. Without a doubt, the most valuable were: *The Registry of the Privy Council of Scotland; History of the Lodge of Edinburgh #1; The Historie of the Life and Death of Mary Stuart Queene of Scotland; Constitutions of the Free Masons; The Life Correspondence Collections of Thomas Howard, Earl of Arundel; When Scotland Was Jewish;* and *Restoring The Temple of Vision.*

I also purchased an exclusive digitalized set of 104 codex sheets created by Mary, Queen of Scots, from the National Archives of the United Kingdom.

•*The Registry of the Privy Council of Scotland* – those volumes regarding the Baronets of Nova Scotia, and spanning the mid-16th through the mid-17th centuries

•*An Encouragement To Colonies,* William Alexander, 1624

•*The Historie of the Life and Death of Mary Stuart Queene of Scotland,* Wil. Stranguage (William Udall), 1624

•*Constitutions of the Free Masons,* James Anderson, 1723

•*Royal Letters, Charters and Tracts Relating to the Colonization of New Scotland and the Institution of the Order of The Knights Baronet of Nova Scotia 1621 – 1638,* The Bannatyne Club, 1827

•*Jewish Literature from the Eighth to the Eighteenth Century,* by Moritz Steinschneider, 1857

• *A History of Nova-Scotia, or Acadie*, James Barnes, 1865

• *The Old Charges of Freemasons*, William Hughan, 1872

• *History of the Lodge of Edinburgh #1*, David Lyon, 1873

• *Memorials of the Earl of Stirling and of the House of Alexander*, Rev. Charles Rogers, 1877

• *The Scottish Master Mason's Handbook*, Frederick Crowe, 1894

• *The Freemason's Repository*, Several Authors, 1897

• *The Life Correspondence Collections of Thomas Howard Earl of Arundel*, Mary F. S. Hervey, 1921

• *Sir William Alexander, First Earl of Stirling*, Thomas McGrail, 1940

• *The Surnames of Scotland*, George Black, 1946

• *The Origins of Freemasonry*, David Stevenson, 1988

• *Freemasonry on Both Sides of the Atlantic*, Richard Weisberger, Wallace McLeod, and S. Brent Morris, 2002

• *Restoring The Temple of Vision*, Marsha Keith Schuchard, 2002

• *Oak Island and Its Lost Treasure*, Graham Harris and Les MacPhie, 2005, revised 2013

• *When Scotland Was Jewish*, Elizabeth C. Hirschman and Donald N. Yates, 2007

Is It Ever Really
The End?

Made in the USA
Middletown, DE
16 February 2023

25033075R00096